PROBLEMS OF THE MODERN ECONOMY

Private Wants and Public Needs

PROBLEMS OF THE MODERN ECONOMY

General Editor: EDMUND S. PHELPS, *Yale University*

Each volume in this series presents
prominent positions in the debate of
an important issue of economic policy

THE BATTLE AGAINST UNEMPLOYMENT

CHANGING PATTERNS IN FOREIGN TRADE AND PAYMENTS

THE GOAL OF ECONOMIC GROWTH

MONOPOLY POWER AND ECONOMIC PERFORMANCE

PRIVATE WANTS AND PUBLIC NEEDS

THE UNITED STATES AND THE DEVELOPING ECONOMIES

Private Wants
and Public Needs

ISSUES SURROUNDING THE SIZE AND
SCOPE OF GOVERNMENT EXPENDITURE

Edited with an introduction by

EDMUND S. PHELPS
YALE UNIVERSITY

NEW YORK
W · W · NORTON & COMPANY · INC ·

Library of Congress Catalog Card No. 62-20922

ALL RIGHTS RESERVED

Published simultaneously in the Dominion of
Canada by George J. McLeod Limited, Toronto.

Standards and Values in a Rich Society, from *The American Economy* by
Alvin H. Hansen. Copyright 1957 by McGraw-Hill Book Company. Reprinted by permission of McGraw-Hill Book Company.

The Dependence Effect and Social Balance, from *The Affluent Society* by
John Kenneth Galbraith. Published by Houghton Mifflin Company. Reprinted by permission of the publishers.

The Non Sequitur of the "Dependence Effect" by F. A. Hayek. From the
Southern Economic Journal (April 1961), pp. 346–348. Reprinted by
permission of the author and the *Southern Economic Journal.*

Public versus Private: Could Galbraith Be Wrong? by Henry C. Wallich.
From *Harper's Magazine* (October 1961) and from *The Cost of Freedom*
by Henry C. Wallich, copyright 1960 by the author. Reprinted by permission of the author and Harper and Row, Publishers.

On State Expenditures, from *The Ethics of Redistribution* by Bertrand de
Jouvenel. Published by the Cambridge University Press. Reprinted by
permission of the publishers.

The "Isms" and Social Technique, originally published as "Social Techniques
and Rational Social Action" from *Politics, Economics and Welfare* by
Robert A. Dahl and Charles E. Lindblom. Copyright 1953 by Harper and
Row, Publishers. Reprinted by permission of the publishers.

The Economic Functions of the State in English Classical Political Economy
from *The Theory of Economic Policy* by Lionel Robbins. Published by
Macmillan and Company Ltd. Reprinted by permission of the author,
the publishers, St. Martin's Press, Inc., and the Macmillan Company of
Canada Ltd.

Government and the Sovereign Consumer, from *The Question of Government
Spending* by Francis M. Bator. Copyright 1960 by the author. Reprinted
by permission of Harper and Row, Publishers.

Prices vs. Taxes: A Classification of U. S. Public Expenditures, from *Public
Finances: Needs, Sources and Utilization* by O. H. Brownlee. Copyright
1961 by the Princeton University Press. Reprinted by permission of the
Princeton University Press.

Acknowledgments

In the preparation of this volume I have benefited from the criticism and
suggestions of many colleagues and students to whom I am grateful. I
would like also to thank Robert Harlow for helping to prepare the list
of further readings, and Mrs. Merle E. Hochman and Mrs. Sally S. Har-
rison for their assistance in preparing the book for publication.

E. S. P.

PRINTED IN THE UNITED STATES OF AMERICA
FOR THE PUBLISHERS BY THE VAIL-BALLOU PRESS, INC.

4 5 6 7 8 9

Contents

Introduction

EVERYONE RECOGNIZES the need for ground rules governing the operation of the private economy. Governments—federal, state, and local—are generally counted on to enforce contracts, sanction private property, outlaw theft, regulate business, and intervene to some degree in the distribution of the yield of private economic activity. It would be wrong to suggest that there are no longer live issues surrounding the performance of these functions. The extent to which governments exert control on the individual is a source of recurrent debate; people do express their continuing interest in the distribution of income, particularly their share in the total tax burden and in the benefits (transfers) disbursed to individuals by the public sector. But if governments confined themselves to carrying out regulatory or housekeeping operations, controversy over the proper role of the public sector in the economy would be far milder than it is today. All production would have to pass the test of market demand. Goods which consumers would not buy would be unprofitable and not be produced. The nation's output would be produced and distributed by private enterprise, for private profit. Every man's employer (neglecting the handful of public employees busy regulating) would be just another private citizen, like himself. In any basic sense, ours would be a "free enterprise" system.

This is not the system we have. Alongside the private-enterprise sector there has grown up a *public sector* that supplies the community with a great many services. To provide these services the public sector now purchases over one-fifth of the Gross National Product—the market value of all goods and services produced by the economy. Whether these public purchases are from private firms who do the producing or whether the public sector employs resources to do its own producing, the consequence is clear: Much of the nation's production is directly determined not by consumer decisions but by government.

These facts will hardly surprise the contemporary observer. Yet the present-day importance of the public sector could hardly have been dreamed of fifty or even twenty-five years ago. The table below describes how rapidly government expenditures and employment have grown.

Expansion of the U.S. Public Sector

	1900	1925	1937	1950	1962
Government expenditures on goods and services (1962 prices)					
In billions of dollars	7.3	20.8	33.4	57.9	117.0
In percent of Gross National Product	9.4	11.3	15.5	15.5	21.2
Government employment					
In millions of persons	1.4	3.2	4.3	8.0	12.0
In percent of total labor force:					
Federal	1.4	1.8	2.2	5.7	7.0
Civilian	1.1	1.4	1.7	3.1	3.1
Military	.3	.4	.5	2.6	3.9
State and Local	3.5	5.3	5.7	6.6	9.1
Total	4.9	7.1	7.9	12.4	16.1

Note.—All 1962 data are preliminary, seasonally adjusted estimates for the first half of the year. Expenditure data are at annual rates.

SOURCES: Solomon Fabricant, *The Trend of Government Activity in the United States since 1900* (National Bureau of Economic Research, 1952); John W. Kendrick, *Productivity Trends in the United States* (National Bureau of Economic Research, 1961); U.S. Department of Commerce, *Survey of Current Business;* U.S. Department of Labor, *Monthly Labor Review.*

And there are contentions heard that the public sector has only begun to fill the need for public services. This remarkable expansion of the public sector and the popular pressures surrounding it have made government expenditures the center of controversy concerning the role of government and public policy. Are public expenditures too large? Too small? By what principles should we decide the magnitude of government expenditures? Is the scope of the existing expenditure programs too broad and an encroachment on private enterprise? Or is the public sector neglecting needs which it alone can effectively satisfy? On what criteria should governments decide whether to supply a service? The essays collected here debate these central questions.

SIZE AND SCOPE OF PUBLIC EXPENDITURE

The volume is divided into two parts. The essays of Part One express a variety of positions on the present size and scope of public expenditures in this country. From the economic view-point, there is on one side the contention that many government expenditures are unnecessary or too large and therefore wasteful of the nation's still-scarce resources; this is countered, on the opposite side, by the argument that while the country is lavishly supplied with private consumer goods, it has skimped irrationally on the kinds of services which can only (or can best) be supplied by government. From the political viewpoint, opposing sides in the debate are taken by those who maintain that the public sector has usurped functions and responsibilities which were better left to the individual business firm, the family, and other valued private institutions, and those who argue that the present range of choices before us is too narrow to pose any grand ideological issues.

One of the most eloquent champions of an expanded role for the public sector is Alvin H. Hansen. His essay calls for a change of values away from materialism and commercialism toward a more intellectually and spiritually satisfying life. Government is viewed as an essential instrument to promote the cultural development of the country. Hansen makes a special plea for greater effort in the field of education. This is essential to raise the "submerged tenth" of the population to a decent standard of living.

Frazar B. Wilde, on the other hand, sees in the rise of government expenditure, particularly Federal expenditures, a tendency to rely on the public sector to meet a widening range of economic needs and fancied ills. Clearly not every problem is best met by Federal spending. Wilde urges that every item in the Federal budget should meet six "tests." After such a scrutiny of the budget, he recommends that some two billion dollars be cut from the budget as an unnecessary expense. Wilde recommends also an accompanying tax reduction; this would channel the released resources to the private sector where spending decisions are made by "people who pay the bills."

A characteristic of both these essays is that they appear to take it for granted that there is something amiss with government spending—that the public is not being well served. Yet it might have been supposed that in our democratic society decisions regarding the public sector serve the best interests of the citizenry.

John Kenneth Galbraith makes explicit his view that the public is being systematically misled into alloting too little to the public sector. He builds most of this argument around what he calls the "dependence effect." As a society becomes affluent, Galbraith argues, wants begin to take on a relative nature: they increase with the increasing capacity to satisfy them. Through the processes of emulation and advertising, wants come to depend on output. Therefore, despite the enormous growth in our capacity to produce, consumers never feel they can release any of this productive capacity, by paying more taxes, for badly needed services. They are caught like mice on a treadmill of ever-growing wants. This irrational response to public needs is reinforced, according to Galbraith, by traditional beliefs that governments are unable to produce anything of economic value. Thus irrationality and tradition conspire to promote what Galbraith regards as a patent imbalance between the public and private sectors. On this sociological evidence Galbraith asserts that economic welfare would be increased more by an expansion of government expenditures than by an expansion of consumer expenditures.

F. A. Hayek takes issue with the dependence-effect argument. All but the most basic wants are conditioned by the cultural environment. But this is no reason to conclude that additional consumer expenditures would be worthless or inferior to public spending. There was no visible demand for the novels of C. P. Snow before they were produced; but this does not make them *ipso facto* of low urgency.

Henry C. Wallich offers another criticism of Galbraith's argument. If consumers spend badly, he argues, then better private spending seems on the face to be indicated, not more government spending—of which there is already quite a little. He asks whether there are not powerful biases—logrolling is an example—working in the opposite direction, toward swollen government budgets. In addition, Wallich objects to the treatment of the public expenditure question as a purely economic problem. Where the product of the public sector is well differentiated from the output of the private sector—such as defense—the question is indeed one of how best to allocate resources among competing ends. But many of the "new needs" are now being satisfied to a degree —and give prospects of being satisfied with increasing effectiveness—by private enterprise. In these cases the question of government spending becomes a political one, a question of competing means, not competing ends. Here the value of freedom must be considered.

Wallich also worries that an expansion of public services in order to meet these new needs would weaken individual incentives to work. In the next essay, George F. Break summarizes his study of the influence of taxation upon the supply of effort. He finds no convincing evidence that high taxes have reduced effort thus far in this country. A possible explanation of this apparent constancy of effort, Break points out, is that a rise of income and sales tax rates exerts two opposing effects on effort: The *substitution* effect tempts the taxpayer to work less because each extra day of work now yields him less additional after-tax buying power. But this is countered by an *income* effect that tempts the taxpayer to work harder and longer at the expense of leisure in order to earn more before-tax income. By earning more he can avoid having to cut his budget for private consumption by the full amount of the tax; he can divide the loss between consumption and leisure so as to lessen its burden. If the income effect is strong enough to offset the substitution effect, then effort, on this theory, will rise rather than fall as a result of a tax-financed government expenditure.*

The essay by Bertrand de Jouvenel extends and elaborates an important argument of Wallich's. As the transfer of functions to the public sector continues, he argues, many private institutions find themselves without responsibilities. A family need no longer support the education of its children; as a result the integrity of the family will suffer, if not education. Patrons of the arts and sciences will no longer be needed, and the diversity and imaginativeness of art and science may be lost in the process.

In the final essay of Part One, Robert A. Dahl and Charles E. Lindblom show that there are a great variety of ways of meeting economic needs even within the public sector. Simple characterizations of this sector as monolithic or coercive will not do. Further, support for public activity no longer comes significantly from socialists. The authors express the belief that decisions regarding the public sector have been safely removed from the

---

* But such an outcome does not imply that society escapes the deadweight welfare loss to which incentive-distorting income and sales taxes generally lead. Ideally all taxes would be unrelated to effort and to consumption so that after-tax wage rates reflected the productivity (in terms of private consumption) of an extra day's work; then public expenditures would have only an income effect tending to increase effort. But governments have to rely mainly on income and sales taxes. Their consequent substitution effect makes effort smaller than it ought to be, whether or not effort rises on balance due to the income effect. Yet the resulting welfare loss may be negligible in relation to the other costs and benefits of public expenditures.

ideological sphere where everything is couched in terms of the grand "isms."

Essential as the debate in Part One is, it raises some unanswered questions. Many of the public needs that have been foremost in the debate would involve the government in new fields of activity. By what criteria should productive tasks be divided between government and business? What makes some needs best satisfied by private enterprise and others best met by the public sector?

Where a task can be filled with equal efficiency by government and by private enterprise, the choice can be made purely on political grounds. In such cases, this country has generally chosen private enterprise. Thus the presence of large government expenditures in our economy, with its pronounced favoring of private enterprise, requires an explanation. Part Two of this volume, which is a brief survey of the developments in "public expenditure theory," helps provide such an explanation.

ECONOMIC FUNCTIONS OF PUBLIC SPENDING

Galbraith stated that the characteristic which distinguishes most goods supplied by the public sector from goods bought by individuals is a "technical one." "The things which could be produced and sold for a price were taken over by private producers. Those that could not, but which were in the end no less urgent for that reason, remained with the state." (p. 42) This statement suggests a number of questions.

How can a good—a commodity or service—be unsaleable despite a market demand for it? Are such unmarketable goods in fact the only kind publicly supplied? Should governments limit themselves to supplying or subsidizing goods which cannot be marketed for a profit? Or are there also goods which can but *should not* be priced for a profit—goods which are equally eligible for government expenditure? If so, what are the characteristics of such goods and how should they be priced? Do national defense and agricultural research share these characteristics? Roads and education? TVA? Television? Telephone? A framework of analysis seems to be needed.

The first selection, by Lionel, Lord Robbins, reveals that the English classical political economists had no articulate theory of the roles of government expenditure. And, far from being doctrinaire concerning the scope of government, the English "classicals" like Smith and Bentham were utilitarian and pragmatic. The only criterion which government activity had to meet was that it promote economic welfare.

Economists are now able to present something like a systematic treatment of the conditions under which governments must intervene, with subsidies and expenditures, if economic welfare is to be maximized. This theory, developed largely by Bowen, Samuelson, and Musgrave, is expounded here by Francis M. Bator. Two types of market failures are considered: the case of decreasing costs, in which private firms cannot break even despite adequate consumer demand, and the case of "public goods"—goods whose consumption is inherently shared, in a well-defined sense. After an exposition of the inability of the private sector to serve the consumer in these cases, Bator examines the kinds of services which governments in the United States actually do provide. He finds that these services are in fact overwhelmingly of such a nature—namely, decreasing cost/public good—that only the public sector can be expected to supply them.

In a related study, O. H. Brownlee allocates all government expenditure programs into three categories: public goods, goods with important "neighborhood," "third-party," or "external" effects, and goods for which at least some price should be charged. (The last category includes most decreasing-cost goods.) Much the same conclusions as Bator's can be drawn. Yet Brownlee emphasizes that while government must subsidize many services, it need not supply all of them free of charge. Nor does the need to finance certain services imply the need of government to administer them. He summarizes the intriguing proposal by Milton Friedman that education be produced and sold privately, with governments merely footing the bill, rather than engaging in the "production" of education.

Walter W. Heller appraises the "theory" of public expenditure presented by Bator and finds it wanting in certain respects. He does not accept, for example, the notion that governments do or should confine themselves to the provision of decreasing-cost or public goods. In many cases, the public provision of certain goods is the most efficient or practicable means to redistribute income. Heller is impressed, like Dahl and Lindblom, with the great variety of responses which government can make to a misallocation of resources in the economy. The economist has to compute and compare the efficiency of each possible response.

Last, George J. Stigler considers the extent to which economic functions assigned to the public sector can be performed adequately by states and localities where grass-roots control is greatest. To what extent are small government units inefficient? How often do the benefits of state and local action spill over boundaries with the result that many local functions are undersupplied from a national viewpoint? Stigler would give each governmental task to the smallest unit which can efficiently perform it.

A few concluding remarks concerning the scope of this volume: We are considering here only government expenditures in the strict sense of the word, that is, only purchases of commodities and services by governmental units and their agencies. This excludes "transfer payments" by governments—payments for which no service has been rendered, to which no strings are attached. To be sure, these transfers raise many of the same issues raised by public expenditures: high taxes, redistribution of income, and so forth. But, unlike expenditures, they do not directly reallocate resources in the economy. Thus they do not interfere with consumer sovereignty, nor with free enterprise in any fundamental sense.

Second, we have not considered the use of government expenditures for anti-cyclical purposes. With respect to combating short-term fluctuations, one can say that this volume is concerned with the average level of government expenditures over the cycle; their variation or timing over the course of the business cycle is another matter. With respect to combating a deeper-seated tendency towards depression, we suppose that measures designed to raise private expenditures, such as tax reductions and easy money, are roughly as effective as increased public expenditures. Similarly, with respect to inflationary tendencies, one has the option to cut private expenditures or public expenditures. Unemployment and inflation depend upon the intensity with which we use (or try to use) our resources, not primarily upon the sector (public or private) where the resources are employed or to which their output is sold. Once the total level of expenditures has been decided, the choice between public and private expenditure must be faced. That is what makes it essentially an economic problem.

PART ONE Private *vs.* Public Spending

Standards and Values in a Rich Society

ALVIN H. HANSEN

Alvin H. Hansen is Lucius N. Littauer Professor of Political Economy Emeritus at Harvard University. His book The American Economy, *in which this essay first appeared, appraises government economic policy in the United States since the war.*

THE ERADICATION OF POVERTY

IT IS not enough to rescue economics, as Keynes sought to do, from the narrow role assigned to it by Marshall—essentially a branch of business cost accounting—and restore it to the loftier plane of Political Economy or, as Adam Smith so aptly put it—The Wealth of Nations. Economics must concern itself with something more than merely maximum output and full employment. It must also concern itself with social priorities. In other words, it must, in a sense, become a branch of moral philosophy, as Adam Smith indeed had it.

In the last half-century the American Economy has lifted the standard of living of the mass population to undreamed-of levels of comfort and luxury. Mass poverty has largely been wiped out.

Income per family in real terms is now about two and a half times as high as at the beginning of this century. This represents a gain in real purchasing power of 1¾ per cent per annum. At the same time working hours have been reduced from around 60 per week to 40 per week; from a ten-hour day and a six-day week to an eight-hour day and a five-day week. The gain in leisure time is clearly one of the best indices of a higher standard of living.

3

Still the impressive rise in purchasing-power income requires at least some qualification. A calculation based on money income and price changes is not altogether convincing. In the nineteenth-century rural society many things were free which we now have to pay for. Consider the amount of labor which must be devoted in modern communities, not to positive productive effort, but to neutralizing the disagreeable consequences of dense concentrations of population in large urban communities. Much effort is devoted, not to providing utilities, but to the removal of disutilities, by-products of industrialization and urbanization. Yet the labor expended on the removal of disutilities is counted in our money economy as a part of our Gross National Product.

Industrialized cities with overcrowded tenement districts have made an effort via public parks to recover *some* of the lost sunshine, open fields, and fresh air formerly enjoyed by rural populations. Yet in many communities the parks are not located where people live, where children can have direct access to them. Instead of big and grand parks we need many small neighborhood parks, not for an outing but for daily use, not for an occasional automobile drive but for continuous recreation.

Thus it is that our ugly industrial cities scarcely help to build up a convincing case that our standard of living is as far above that of fifty or a hundred years ago as the figures of money incomes corrected for price changes would indicate. In 1900, 60 per cent of our population lived in rural areas and only 22 per cent in cities of over 25,000. Now only 40 per cent live in rural areas, and 60 million people live in cities of over 25,000. The terrific problems of providing urban transportation involve a vast investment of capital and labor. And while the work week is far shorter, should we not add back some part of the hours spent in the nerve-racking rush to get to and from work? In these terms there are still many people who have what in fact amounts to a ten-hour day.

HOUSING AND EDUCATION

The American people are certainly better housed now than fifty years ago. Plumbing, electric lights, and central heating are indicative of this advance. Yet even today we have over 7 million substandard dwelling units which ought at once to be demolished, either because they are without toilet, bath, running water, or are otherwise dilapidated. Kerosene stoves still heat a high proportion of the homes in many working-class sections—a major cause of fires. To complete the task of raising housing standards to the minimum of decency for all would require, it is estimated by the Twentieth Century Fund,[1] around $85 billion. There is still a good deal of unfinished business before we can say that the American people are well housed. Nonetheless, there is a vast difference between the housing facilities available to the American wage-earning family today compared with the situation around 1890, when Jacob Riis gave his lurid description of *How the Other Half Lives*.

So familiar have we become with the widespread use of electrical household appliances that we are prone to think that all Americans are now equipped with these comforts. Yet 50 per cent do not have vacuum cleaners, 30 per cent do not have electric washing machines, and 20 per cent are without electric refrigerators.[2] Still, apart from food and housing and more leisure time, the most conspicuous gains, no doubt, for the great majority are the mechanical gadgets, comforts, and luxuries—household appliances, plumbing, the automobile, the motion picture, radio, and television.

The substitution of mechanical power for human power and the consequent gains in productivity have not only reduced the work week from 60 to 40 hours; they have also made possible a much longer period of education for the whole population. In this respect we have witnessed a truly revolutionary development since 1900, indeed since 1910. As late as 1910 only 5 per cent of the youth of college age (18 to 21) attended college. By 1950 it was 30 per cent.[3] As late as 1910 only a few went on to high school. Then the flood began. Already by 1920 high-school graduations per capita had doubled, and by 1940 the number graduating from high school each year was, per capita, eight times that of 1900. And by 1950 the number of graduations from colleges

1. *America's Needs and Resources*, Twentieth Century Fund, 1955, p. 512.

2. *Ibid.*, p. 242.

3. James B. Conant, *Education and Liberty*, Harvard University, 1953, p. 35.

and universities, on a per capita basis, had reached eight times that of 1900.

Nothing else like it has occurred in any other part of the world. We have not had time to make the proper adjustments. This flood of students into secondary schools and higher institutions has come upon us in a single generation. It is no wonder that our high-school standards are low. No nation could train an adequate number of competent teachers in so short a time. Worse yet, we have miserably failed to give teachers the salary differential needed to draw the best brains into the teaching profession. On the stage we ridicule schoolma'ams, and in the market place we underprice them.

The task of education is, moreover, enormously complicated by the heterogeneity of our population and the difficult problem of immigrant adjustment to American life. Forty-five million immigrants have stormed our shores during the last hundred years. In 1900, 40 per cent of the whole population was foreign-born, or born of foreign parents, and the figure is still 25 per cent today.

THE SUBMERGED TENTH

This mass immigration explains in no small measure the extraordinary spread between the median income in the United States and the income of the lowest decile. And it accounts in considerable degree for many personal and family maladjustments and social dislocations.

What was it that caused this massive movement of people from the Old World to the New? It was primarily the revolutionary increase in population which occurred in Europe throughout the nineteenth century. From 1800 to 1910 the population of the five largest European countries—England, France, Italy, Germany, and Russia—increased from 125 million to 325 million. The chief cause was the sharp decline in the death rate. The struggle for existence grew desperate. Subdivision of the family plots pushed down the subsistence level. Peasants by the millions were forced off the land. In America they crowded, after the 1880s, into our great urban industrial centers. Uprooted from their Old World peasant communities, where human ties were close and moral values were firmly fixed, they were all at sea in a new and strange world. The uprooted immigrant had to readjust his peasant outlook on life.[4] He had to come to terms with an urbanized industrialism.

To make matters still worse, a psychological conflict, placing severe strains on parental discipline, inevitably developed between the immigrant and his children—a conflict born of differences in language and social environment. The restraints and security of the Old World peasant communities were missing. Sheds, shanties, stables, and cellars were drafted for living space in our great industrial centers. The crowded street was the only playground.[5] Out of such conditions have grown psychopathic disorders and social maladjustments. It is true that those endowed with exceptional energy and capacity, both mental and physical, found in the American environment almost boundless opportunities and rose very rapidly to higher social and economic levels. More gradually the great middle group also improved its status and succeeded reasonably well in the difficult process of amalgamation and assimilation. But there was also the submerged tenth or quintile.

The physical and mental deficiencies which we find today among the lower two deciles of our population stem in part at least from the conflicts experienced by the uprooted peasant immigrant unable to find his way about in congested cities amid the uncertainties and insecurity of a laissez-faire industrialism. Against the background of these conditions one can learn a good deal that explains the submerged decile in a rich society.

In the United States today there are 8,000,000 families and individual household units with a money income of less than $1,000 per year and an additional 6,500,000 with incomes between $1,000 and $2,000. A considerable proportion live in depressed areas, where unemployment is chronic even when the nation as a whole is enjoying full-employment opportunities. It is a vicious circle. Because the area is depressed, public revenues are limited. Community services, and especially the quality of education, are seriously deficient. Such areas become not merely economi-

---

4. Oscar Handlin, *The Uprooted,* Little, Brown & Company, 1952.
5. I note even today, as I walk around the streets of some of our great cities, that school children in recess time have frequently no place to play except on pavement and adjoining sidewalks.

cally depressed areas; they become also derelict areas, composed of a population with inferior education and lacking in physical and mental vigor. The able, aggressive young people migrate. Those who remain behind constitute, disproportionately, aged persons, remaining members of broken families, and generally persons inadequately equipped to compete successfully in modern industry.

In part it is a rural problem, and in part it is a race problem. Two-thirds of the low-income rural families live in the South. Moreover, the incidence of low incomes among rural families is twice as great among Negroes as among whites.

Lack of education is a primary cause of low income. Low-income families are compelled to spend a disproportionate per cent of their income on food and housing. There is little left for education. Substandard families spend 65 per cent of their income on food and housing, while wage-earning families in general spend only 45 per cent on these two consumption categories. Moreover, as I have already indicated, such families are likely to live in communities where educational facilities are very limited. About 30 per cent of all the nation's children live in the eighteen lowest-income states. Several of these states have a per capita income less than half that of the richest states.

These poorer states cannot, without substantial Federal aid, provide the minimum American standards of education, health, and social welfare. These children are Americans. Yet citizens of New York and Massachusetts are prone to talk and act as though they were foreigners. We are indeed almost immeasurably distant from being *world* citizens. In the present stage of human development this is at least understandable. But is it not incredible that we pretend to be citizens of our separate states and not citizens of the United States when we consider the problem of adequate minimum standards of education for Americans everywhere?

The wide spread between the median income and the lowest decile in our society holds not only with respect to income and education but also with respect to physical fitness. Not only is the rate of illiteracy high in the lower deciles, but the extraordinary high proportion of our total youth physically and mentally unfit for military service is clearly in some part to be explained by the unfavorable economic and social conditions under which the lower deciles of our population live. Slum clearance and a nationwide system of health insurance are high in the agenda of unfinished business.

It is not only the personal incomes and the physical and mental status of the submerged tenth which are seriously deficient. It is also their opportunity to share in the amenities of life which only the community can offer. Our great cities lack adequate parks and playgrounds—Cambridge, Mass., is a notorious example—and they lack community facilities for recreation and social life. The joy of living in a city with beautiful parks within the reach of all and with easy and quick access to the surrounding countryside is something that our lower-income groups do not share in equal measure with comparable income groups in Holland, Switzerland, Denmark, and Sweden.

Joyful living is not simply an individual matter. Among the more important amenities of life are those which only the community can provide. This is a job for government. And if we hide behind the doctrine that all this is no affair of the Federal government, we become in practice pure defeatists.

The lower-income classes are at a peculiar disadvantage because of the preoccupation of the American society with mechanical gadgets and because of the relatively slight emphasis placed upon social values and community activities. We are increasingly in danger of making our economic system a mere treadmill. We have reached a point in our development where mere emphasis on larger and larger output of mechanical gadgets becomes rather meaningless, if, indeed, not a detriment to truly satisfactory living. We spend billions and billions of dollars on automobiles, of which perhaps half is frittered away on mere size, gadgets, and chrome—all of which add little to the social utility of comfortable transportation. And expenditures on automobiles, not including operation or the vast sums spent on roads, are twice as great as the aggregate expenditure on schools, including school construction and other capital outlays for education.

The average public-school teacher's salary is $3,450, while the average full-time wage for production workers in manufacturing industry is $3,735, and that for railroad production workers (not including supervising employees) is $4,100. A country as rich as ours can and should make the school teacher's profession highly attractive financially. A good rule, and a thoroughly justifiable one, would be an average salary scale twice that of production workers. This means more than a doubling of school teachers' salaries. In ten years we should see a profound change in the quality of our teachers. To say that we can't afford it is nonsense. We are spending currently a paltry $3½ billion on public-school teachers' salaries. We can well afford to double or treble that amount out of our rapidly increasing national income.

We shall not solve the problem of education for the submerged tenth or the lowest quintile until we have solved it for all the people. The same holds for youth programs, recreational facilities, and a nationwide system of health insurance.

WHAT GOALS DO WE SEEK?

After ten years of almost incredible *output* performance, we need to assess not merely the speed of our growth and progress but also the direction in which we are going. What *qualitative* goals shall we set up? What kind of country do we wish to build? These are matters that we dare not overlook, lest we perish, as a great nation, in the midst of material plenty.

Now someone will surely say: "What right has this armchair professor to talk about how the American public should use its resources? Leave it to the market to take care of all that." Superficially that sounds good, but in fact that answer will not do. The "market" cannot decide how much we shall spend on schools, on social security, or on national security. We have reached a point in our economic and social evolution where *social-value* judgments, not the market, must control the uses to which we put something like one-fourth of our productive resources. Our economy is no longer wholly a market economy. It is a mixed public-private economy.

And how are these social-value judgments to be determined? Do we leave it to chance, to nature, to the elemental, uneducated instincts of people? That indeed is the rule among savages. But civilized countries follow another rule, and it is this: "Train up a child in the way he should go, and when he is a man he will not depart therefrom." Civilized countries mold their people into civilized ways of thinking, guided by values that experience and knowledge have laid down. We don't leave it to the market. We educate. Only in this way can we achieve the great goals of a civilized society.

Here I come to a critical point. Our schools and churches can no longer be said to constitute the main educational media in this country. Modern technology has largely supplanted these older media. Children, young people, and grownups devote more hours per day the year round to the radio and television and the movies than they do to school, churches, or to reading. These mechanical media have become an important, if indeed not the most important, element in our entire educational process. And what worries me is this. These powerful educational media are controlled, not by educators, but by advertisers whose primary purpose is profit, not education. Advertisers do not control the editorials or news columns of our newspapers, though there may be an indirect influence. But they do control our radio and television programs. Is it any wonder that we prefer longer and longer cars with more and more chrome to good schools and well-paid teachers? At the very least, advertisers should not, I suggest, be allowed to sponsor or select the programs other than their own commercials.

We have been brought up with a narrow conception of the functions of public education. Adult education, music, drama, the fine arts, deserve public support. Even our F.M. fine music programs are painfully encroached upon by advertising.

Thus the problem of social priorities is hard upon us. It is not enough to achieve maximum employment and production. It is not enough to have quantitative goals. We cannot allow full employment to become merely a device to make our economy an efficient treadmill.

America's Needs and Resources discloses (p. 512) that the estimated cost of urban redevelopment in general—including a demolition of our 7 million slum houses—would amount to no more than the equivalent of about two years of defense expenditures at current levels.

In terms of GNP we are spending currently only 40 per cent as much on hospitals today as in 1920–1924 (p. 312). We are spending (including operating and capital expenditures) only

2¼ per cent of our GNP on public schools, elementary and secondary. Indeed, in relation to GNP we are spending 20 per cent
less on schools today than we spent twenty-five years ago. A rich
country can't afford good schools and good teachers!

This is an area in which economists have been, I feel, neglectful
of their duty. We need more study of social priorities.

Yet with all our distorted values there is happily a growing
realization that we *have* accumulated a large backlog of long-
range public-investment needs. This means larger and larger
Federal budgets, not only absolutely but also in relation to the
GNP. When I say "public investment" I mean not merely public
works and resource-development projects. I include investment
in human resources as well—schools, scholarship programs, medical research, a nationwide system of health insurance, recreational
facilities, etc.

The problem of long-range public-investment planning is all
the more important in view of our large and now again increasing
defense and foreign-aid budgets. The national-security budgets
compete with the growing urgent need for much larger long-
range social-welfare budgets. I think we should all agree that
national security comes first. Indeed I have never been able to
understand why we continually debate the question whether
our military strength is more or less equal to that of the Soviet
Union when we, in fact, have ample resources to ensure our
superiority by a wide margin. Our military program should be
adequate to guarantee without question the peace of the world
for the visible future. I am not, therefore, suggesting that we
should reduce our military program. But I do, nonetheless, say
that we should increase *now* by a substantial amount our long-
range public-welfare budgets. That may involve a reappraisal
of tax cuts. We are in a situation in which the marginal *tax* dollar
can clearly yield a much higher social utility than the marginal
pay-envelope dollar.

Let it be noted that the growing ratio of government purchases
of goods and services—a trend which has been going on throughout our history—does indeed point up the unmistakable *fact* that
our economy is becoming more and more a mixed public-private
economy. But government ownership and operation of the means
of production—the classical definition of socialism—is *not* no-

ticeably on the increase. It is the welfare state that is growing, not the government as owner or operator. The welfare state is primarily a redistributor of income and a colossal purchaser of the products of private enterprise. But private enterprise does the job.

The growth of public budgets means that the public *finance* method of paying for goods and services will grow in relation to the *market-price* method. It does not mean that private enterprise is shrinking or that the tax base is shrinking. The goods are purchased from private enterprise. Thus private enterprise continues to grow in much the same proportion as the GNP. The welfare state does not in any appreciable degree operate to supplant the system of private enterprise. Instead it makes it stronger and more workable.

No one can dispute that we have become a rich society. We have made great advances on the purely economic plane. Unfortunately the progress we have made in many of the noneconomic aspects of life is limited, and in some areas we have, I fear, definitely retrogressed. The economic gains are visible on every hand. And economists, as a professional group, have, I think it is fair to say, contributed in no small measure to this development. Government departments have at long last been staffed with well-trained economists. State papers nowadays are mainly concerned with economic matters, often highly technical. Congressional hearings and legislative programs draw increasingly on the work of economists inside and outside the government. The result is evident in the massive and highly technical messages and reports of the President to Congress.

Would that our colleagues, concerned with noneconomic aspects of American life, could claim equal progress. We are learning, in the midst of material plenty, that man "cannot live by bread alone." How do educators feel when they contemplate the deterioration of our public schools; the social psychologists and pathologists who observe the increase in mental disorders, crime, and juvenile delinquency, or, on another plane, the current predominance of neurotic art?

We have learned how to make a living; we have still to learn how to live. Until we have eliminated the ugliness of our great industrial cities we cannot claim to have reached as a nation a truly high standard of living. America is long on wealth but short on appreciation of the beautiful. Some years ago I visited, in company with Professor Jørgen Pedersen, a large farm in Jutland, Denmark. It employed eighteen or twenty well-housed farm workers. Two of these devoted full time to beautifying the place, to the flower gardens, the lawns, the trees, the buildings. That farm was a place on which to live, not merely a place to make a living.

Many readers have no doubt visited the famous Town Hall in Stockholm, a noble work of man. Compare this with the city hall in Boston, Mass., to take only one example. The Town Hall in Stockholm is not simply a place where the mayor has his office. It is a community building where citizens of high or low rank can meet in civic-group gatherings amidst an atmosphere of dignity, beauty, and elegance. Such things make for the good life. A higher standard of mere material wealth is no substitute for beauty—for the things of the mind and the spirit.

Few will deny the cultural deficiencies of our cities and towns, and everyone will agree that an adequate program would cost a lot of money. And the answer to that usually is that we can't afford it. We are too poor! Ah, that is it. We have become so gadget-rich that we can't afford to build culturally rich communities. But what does it profit a man if he gain the whole world but lose his own soul?

A Proposal to Reduce Federal Expenditures

FRAZAR B. WILDE

Frazar B. Wilde is the Chairman of the Policy Council of the Committee for Economic Development. The CED is a group of business leaders which supports professional research and makes policy recommendations concerning current economic problems. Wilde contributed this paper in hearings on government expenditures held by the Joint Economic Committee of the U.S. Congress.

IN POPULAR cartoons, the budget cutter is often pictured as a little, shortsighted, narrowminded man brandishing an ax in a reckless attempt to cut the Government back to the size of 1890. The budget issue is described as an issue between outmoded financial dogmas and modern human and national needs.

For myself and for the CED I want to disclaim this caricature and deny that this is the true issue. In a series of policy statements issued in the past 15 years CED has demonstrated its awareness of national needs and government responsibilities in the twentieth century. Precisely because we are concerned with the second half of the twentieth century we in the CED are alarmed by a trend of rapidly rising Federal expenditure that has gone on through peace and war, through depression, prosperity and inflation, through Democratic and Republican administrations. We believe that this trend is dangerous to the efficient, dynamic, decentralized and free society upon which we must rely to meet the needs and aspirations of the American people.

We have in this country a highly effective society for meeting national needs. This society includes the private economy, voluntary associations of all kinds, as well as all state and local governments and the Federal Government. It is not a denial of the existence of needs to say that they should not be met by Federal spending. It is a denial that every problem, every need, every felt want is best met by Federal spending. It is a plea for maximum reliance upon the other elements of our society.

There are strong arguments for keeping reliance upon Federal spending to a minimum. Spending decisions will be more eco-

nomical and efficient if they are made directly by the people who
pay the bills. The economy will grow more rapidly if the investment of savings must meet the test of profitability in a competitive market. The freedom of the individual will be more
assured the more limited is the size and power of the central
government. Last but not least, we can help avoid inflationary
pressures by holding down the size of the national budget.

The unfairness with which the burden of Government spending
is distributed among the people is not fully recognized. I do not
refer here simply to the nominal distribution of taxation, which
is bad enough. But the legal imposition of taxes does not determine the final allocation of the burden. Individuals and businesses
differ greatly in their ability to escape the burden by passing it
on in higher wages and prices. Those with weakest bargaining
and market power pay not only their own taxes but also the taxes
of others, in the form of reduced real incomes. The inflation we
have been experiencing has been partly, in my opinion, a process
of passing on the costs of government. This is especially likely to
be true when Government programs, like parts of the defense
program, are pushed with a speed that is bound to be inflationary.

These arguments obviously do not rule out all Federal expenditure. There are functions that only the Federal Government can
perform, and today these are large and expensive functions. But
every Federal function and expenditure must be rigorously and
critically examined in the light of these strong arguments. This
has not been done. Introduction of new programs and expansion
of old ones has been accepted as a matter of course, as a remedy
for every real or fancied ill. Programs have been adopted without knowledge of their ultimate cost and scale. Various programs
have been advanced by the influence of particular groups that
have special interests in them. And the whole process of increased
spending has been facilitated by the automatic increase in tax
revenues from our growing economy, which has permitted larger
expenditures to be financed by higher tax rates.

As a practical matter, the way the democratic process functions
at the present time, there is no adequate balancing force to the
aggressive demands of well-organized groups.

I am not at all impressed by the argument that because our
economy is growing we need or should have larger Federal expenditures. This argument is probably valid for some objects of
expenditure, such as roads. But it is certainly not true of many

other expenditures. In fact, one would expect that as people become more prosperous, the need for many Government expenditures would decline. Rising private incomes and employment opportunities should enable us to spend less on such things as aid to agriculture, housing subsidies, and public assistance. But we don't. We used to be told that the Federal Government had to spend large sums because the private economy was not working well and because people were poor. Now it appears that we must spend even larger sums because the economy is thriving.

In any case, the point is not whether the total Federal expenditures are now a larger or smaller proportion of the gross national product than they were in some earlier year. The point is whether all the particular expenditures that are proposed are necessary. We believe that many of them are not.

HOW TO CUT THE BUDGET

Every item in the Federal budget should be tested by six questions:
1. Is there a real need?
2. Must the need be met by Government?
3. Must the need be met by Federal Government?
4. Does Federal spending meet the need?
5. Is the Federal spending program efficient?
6. Must the spending be done now?

In our policy statement we consider a number of major programs and suggest reasons for believing that they do not fully meet these tests. For example, we question whether the mortgage purchase program is meeting a need that must be met by Government. We suggest that Federal grants for public assistance have exceeded the proper responsibilities of the Federal Government. We point to the failure of Federal spending for aid to agriculture to solve the basic farm problem. The agricultural program has been self-defeating because it is too large and it has demonstrated that it fails to meet the practical problems of agriculture in a free society. We question whether our defense program is efficient, either in the sense of the suitability of our plans to our requirements or in the sense of the economy with which the plans are executed. We recommend that some of the proposed public works projects should be deferred or even eliminated.

We do not favor a meat-axe approach to budget cutting. Some

functions are vital and should not be cut. Some may need expansion. The meat-axe is an instrument of despair, and only justified if it is impossible to get the information and cooperation needed for a discriminating cut.

*Suggestions for Cutting Nondefense Expenditures
in Fiscal Year 1958*

Program	Amount of reduction	Remarks
FNMA secondary mortgage purchase program.	*Millions* $500	This program was intended to alleviate temporary shortages of mortgages, not to insulate the mortgage market from general monetary policy. The proposed cut would reduce FNMA purchases under this program to the 1956 level. There would be little need for additional Federal funds if Federal agencies that insure and guarantee mortgages were given the authority to meet the mortgage rates prevailing in the market place.
Postponement of public works construction.	450	This would cut in half the projected increase in Federal construction (other than highways) between fiscal years 1957 and 1958. A slowing down of Federal construction is desirable so long as the demands for nongovernmental needs remain high.
Agricultural Conservation Service.	230	This program in effect shares with the farmers the cost of many current outlays for crop cultivation. By encouraging farmers to increase production, this program is actually in conflict with other agricultural programs, like the conservation reserve and the soil bank, which are intended to promote a reduction of farm production. Elimination of this program would not have any effect on the soil conservation program, which was designed as a long-run conservation measure. In addition to this step, the permissible price support levels should be lowered for future crops, but such action would have little effect on the fiscal 1958 budget.

Program	Amount of reduction	Remarks
Improvement of airways facilities.	200	A system of user charges should be developed to pay for the estimated increase in expenditures between fiscal years 1956 and 1958 for the improvement of airway facilities. This is consistent with a recommendation made by the President in the budget message and repeated in his letter to the Speaker dated Apr. 18, 1957.
Federal aid for school construction.	185	This is a proposed Federal program which will eventually cost at least $2 billion. CED has not studied the evidence sufficiently to determine whether there is need for Federal aid in this area. It is my personal opinion that this program should be deferred and restudied.
Stockpiling and other mineral purchase programs.	175	Current plans call for purchases of minerals amounting to $350 million in fiscal year 1958. Much of the program has little defense justification but has become a means of price support.
Veterans' benefits	100	This would eliminate the proposed increase for implementing the Bradley Commission recommendations. The necessary reforms to improve the equity of veterans' payments should be financed by lowering excessive payments for non-service-connected illnesses and disabilities.
Federal aid for the construction of waste treatment facilities.	60	This is a program for Federal aid in an area which should be reserved entirely to the local and/or State governments, since sewage disposal is a local problem.
Area assistance	10	This program, which is intended to assist depressed areas, should not be financed with Federal funds. Although estimated expenditures in the fiscal year are small, this is the type of program that is likely to become very large once it is permanently established.

NOTE.—Total estimated reduction in cash expenditures in fiscal year 1958, $1,910 million.

Cutting and controlling the budget requires cutting and controlling programs. Something can be done, always, by increasing efficiency. But basically we must get at the number and kinds of things the Government does and the scale on which it does them. This is not going to be easy. There is nothing in the budget that somebody doesn't want.

In this connection one of the major changes which the Congress needs to adopt is the item veto. Any program which meets the test of real need is not likely to suffer an item veto and, if it did, it could be passed over the veto.

I have attached to this statement a table listing cuts in fiscal year 1958 nondefense cash expenditures amounting to almost $2 billion. These cuts are consistent with the general principles listed by CED in its recent policy statement, but I want to emphasize that the specific suggestions reflect only my personal views.

If such cuts were made they would permit enactment of a moderate tax cut to take effect at the beginning of 1958. They would raise the 1958 cash surplus to over $5 billion and would give promise of a continued surplus in later years.

We are now confronted with a Federal budget which has grown enormously without critical examination or any attempt at over-all coordination. We have tended to accept it on the basis that it was either the result of past wars or necessary to prevent new ones. Realistic consideration of the budget shows that we are excusing ourselves and are not facing issues squarely.

The Dependence Effect and Social Balance

JOHN KENNETH GALBRAITH

John Kenneth Galbraith, formerly Professor of Economics at Harvard University, is now United States Ambassador to India. In The Affluent Society, *from which the following essay is taken, Galbraith examines the use to which this country puts its wealth.*

WEALTH IS not without its advantages and the case to the contrary, although it has often been made, has never proved widely persuasive. But, beyond doubt, wealth is the relentless enemy of understanding. The poor man has always a precise view of his problem and its remedy: he hasn't enough and he needs more. The rich man can assume or imagine a much greater variety of ills and he will be correspondingly less certain of their remedy. Also, until he learns to live with his wealth, he will have a well-observed tendency to put it to the wrong purposes or otherwise to make himself foolish.

As with individuals so with nations. And the experience of nations with well-being is exceedingly brief. Nearly all throughout all history have been very poor. The exception, almost insignificant in the whole span of human existence, has been the last few generations in the comparatively small corner of the world populated by Europeans. Here, and especially in the United States, there has been great and quite unprecedented affluence.

The ideas by which the people of this favored part of the world interpret their existence, and in measure guide their behavior, were not forged in a world of wealth. These ideas were the product of a world in which poverty had always been man's normal lot, and any other state was in degree unimaginable. This poverty was not the elegant torture of the spirit which comes from contemplating another man's more spacious possessions. It was the unedifying mortification of the flesh—from hunger, sickness, and cold. Those who might be freed temporarily from such burden could not know when it would strike again, for at best hunger yielded only perilously to privation. It is improbable that the poverty of the masses of the people was made greatly more bearable by the fact that a very few—those upon whose movements nearly all recorded history centers—were very rich.

No one would wish to argue that the ideas which interpreted this world of grim scarcity would serve equally well for the contemporary United States. Poverty was the all-pervasive fact of that world. Obviously it is not of ours. One would not expect that the preoccupations of a poverty-ridden world would be relevant in one where the ordinary individual has access to amenities—foods, entertainment, personal transportation, and plumbing—in which not even the rich rejoiced a century ago. So great has been the change that many of the desires of the individual are no longer even evident to him. They become so only as they are synthesized, elaborated, and nurtured by advertising and salesmanship, and these, in turn, have become among our most important and talented professions. Few people at the beginning of the nineteenth century needed an adman to tell them what they wanted.

It would be wrong to suggest that the economic ideas which once interpreted the world of mass poverty have made no adjustment to the world of affluence. There have been many adjustments including some that have gone unrecognized or have been poorly understood. But there has also been a remarkable resistance. And the total alteration in underlying circumstances has not been squarely faced. As a result we are guided, in part, by ideas that are relevant to another world; and as a further result we do many things that are unnecessary, some that are unwise, and a few that are insane. . . .

THE LOW REPUTE OF PUBLIC PRODUCTION

Our concern for production is traditional and irrational. We are curiously unreasonable in the distinctions we make between different kinds of goods and services. We view the production of some of the most frivolous goods with pride. We regard the production of some of the most significant and civilizing services with regret.

In the general view it is privately produced production that is important, and that nearly alone. This adds to national well-being. Its increase measures the increase in national wealth.

Public services, by comparison, are an incubus. They are necessary, and they may be necessary in considerable volume. But
they are a burden which must, in effect, be carried by the private
production. If that burden is too great, private production will
stagger and fall.

At best public services are a necessary evil; at worst they
are a malign tendency against which an alert community must
exercise eternal vigilance. Even when they serve the most important ends, such services are sterile. "Government is powerless
to create anything in the sense in which business produces
wealth. . . ."[1]

Such attitudes lead to some interesting contradictions. Automobiles have an importance greater than the roads on which they
are driven. We welcome expansion of telephone services as improving the general well-being but accept curtailment of postal
services as signifying necessary economy. We set great store by
the increase in private wealth but regret the added outlays for
the police force by which it is protected. Vacuum cleaners to
insure clean houses are praiseworthy and essential in our standard
of living. Street cleaners to insure clean streets are an unfortunate
expense. Partly as a result, our houses are generally clean and our
streets generally filthy. In the more sophisticated of the conventional wisdom, this distinction between public and private
services is much less sharp and, as I have observed, it does not
figure in the calculation of Gross National Product. However, it
never quite disappears. Even among economists and political
philosophers, public services rarely lose their connotation of
burden. Although they may be defended, their volume and
quality are almost never a source of pride.

There are a number of reasons for these attitudes, but again
tradition plays a dominant role. In the world into which economics was born the four most urgent requirements of man were
food, clothing, and shelter, and an orderly environment in which
the first three might be provided. The first three lent themselves
to private production for the market; given good order, this
process has ordinarily gone forward with tolerable efficiency.
But order which was the gift of government was nearly always

1. Francis X. Sutton, Seymour E. Harris, Carl Kaysen, and James Tobin,
The American Business Creed (Cambridge, Mass.: Harvard University Press,
1956), p. 195.

supplied with notable unreliability. With rare exceptions it was also inordinately expensive. And the pretext of providing order not infrequently afforded the occasion for rapacious appropriation of the means of sustenance of the people.

Not surprisingly, modern economic ideas incorporated a strong suspicion of government. The goal of nineteenth century economic liberalism was a state which did provide order reliably and inexpensively and which did as little as possible else. Even Marx intended that the state should wither away. These attitudes have persisted in the conventional wisdom. And again events have dealt them a series of merciless blows. Once a society has provided itself with food, clothing, and shelter, all of which so fortuitously lend themselves to private production, purchase, and sale, its members begin to desire other things. And a remarkable number of these things do not lend themselves to such production, purchase, and sale. They must be provided for everyone if they are to be provided for anyone, and they must be paid for collectively or they cannot be had at all. Such is the case with streets and police and the general advantages of mass literacy and sanitation, the control of epidemics, and the common defense. There is a bare possibility that the services which must be rendered collectively, although they enter the general scheme of wants after the immediate physical necessities, increase in urgency more than proportionately with increasing wealth. This is more likely if increasing wealth is matched by increasing population and increasing density of population. Nonetheless these services, although they reflect increasingly urgent desires, remain under the obloquy of the unreliability, incompetence, cost, and pretentious interference of princes. Alcohol, comic books, and mouth wash all bask under the superior reputation of the market. Schools, judges, and municipal swimming pools lie under the evil reputation of bad kings.

Moreover, bad kings in a poorer world showed themselves to be quite capable, in their rapacity, of destroying or damaging the production of private goods by destroying the people and the capital that produced them. Economies are no longer so vulnerable. Governments are not so undiscriminating. In western countries in modern times economic growth and expanding public activity have, with rare exceptions, gone together. Each has served the other as indeed they must. Yet the conventional wisdom is far from surrendering on the point. Any growth in public services is a manifestation of an intrinsically evil trend. If the vigor of the race is not in danger, liberty is. And this may be threatened even by the activities of the local school board. The structure of the economy may also be at stake. In one branch of the conventional wisdom the American economy is never far removed from socialism, and the movement toward socialism may be measured by the rise in public spending. Thus even the most neutral of public services, for one part of the population, fall under the considerable handicap of being identified with social revolution.

Finally—also a closely related point—the payment for publicly produced services has long been linked to the problem of inequality. By having the rich pay more, the services were provided and at the same time the goal of greater equality was advanced. This community of objectives has never appealed to those being equalized. Not unnaturally, some part of their opposition has been directed to the public services themselves. By attacking these, they could attack the leveling tendencies of taxation. This has helped to keep alive the notion that the public services for which they pay are inherently inferior to privately produced goods.

While public services have been subject to these negative attitudes, private goods have had no such attention. On the contrary, their virtues have been extolled by the massed drums of modern advertising. They have been pictured as the ultimate wealth of the community. Clearly the competition between public and private services, apart from any question of the satisfactions they render, is an unequal one. The social consequences of this discrimination—this tendency to accord a superior prestige to private goods and an inferior role to public production—are considerable and even grave.

THE IMPERATIVES OF CONSUMER DEMAND

Both the ancient preoccupation with production and the pervasive modern search for security have culminated in our time in a concern for production. Increased real income provides us with an admirable detour around the rancor anciently associated with efforts to redistribute wealth. A high level of production has become the keystone of effective economic security. There remains, however, the task of justifying the resulting flow of goods. Production cannot be an incidental to the mitigation of inequality or the provision of jobs. It must have a *raison d'être* of its own. At this point economists and economic theory have entered the game. The result has been an elaborate and ingenious defense of the importance of production as such. It is a defense which makes the urgency of production largely independent of the volume of production. In this way economic theory has managed to transfer the sense of urgency in meeting consumer need that once was felt in a world where more production meant more food for the hungry, more clothing for the cold, and more houses for the homeless to a world where increased output satisfies the craving for more elegant automobiles, more exotic food, more erotic clothing, more elaborate entertainment—indeed for the entire modern range of sensuous, edifying, and lethal desires.

Although the economic theory which defends these desires and hence the production that supplies them has an impeccable (and to an astonishing degree even unchallenged) position in the conventional wisdom, it is illogical and meretricious and in degree even dangerous. . . .

In part [the defense by economists] will take the form of a purely assertive posture. "There is still an economic problem"; "We still have poverty"; "It is human nature to want more"; "Without increasing production there will be stagnation"; "We must show the Russians." But the ultimate refuge will remain in the theory of consumer demand. This is a formidable structure; it has already demonstrated its effectiveness in defending the urgency of production. In a world where affluence is rendering the old ideas obsolete, it will continue to be the bastion against the misery of new ones.

The theory of consumer demand, as it is now widely accepted, is based on two broad propositions, neither of them quite explicit but both extremely important for the present value system of economists. The first is that the urgency of wants does not diminish appreciably as more of them are satisfied or, to put the matter more precisely, to the extent that this happens it is not demonstrable and not a matter of any interest to economists or for economic policy. When man has satisfied his physical needs, then psychologically grounded desires take over. These can never be satisfied or, in any case, no progress can be proved. The concept of satiation has very little standing in economics. It is neither useful nor scientific to speculate on the comparative cravings of the stomach and the mind.

The second proposition is that wants originate in the personality of the consumer or, in any case, that they are given data for the economist. The latter's task is merely to seek their satisfaction. He has no need to inquire how these wants are formed. His function is sufficiently fulfilled by maximizing the goods that supply the wants.

The examination of these two conclusions must now be pressed. The explanation of consumer behavior has its ancestry in a much older problem, indeed the oldest problem of economics, that of price determination.[2] Nothing originally proved more troublesome in the explanation of prices, i.e., exchange values, than the indigestible fact that some of the most useful things had the least value in exchange and some of the least useful had the most. As Adam Smith observed: "Nothing is more useful than water; but it will purchase scarce anything; scarce anything can be had in exchange for it. A diamond, on the contrary, has scarce any value in use: but a very great quantity of other goods may frequently be had in exchange for it."[3]

In explaining value, Smith thought it well to distinguish between "value in exchange" and "value in use" and sought thus to reconcile the paradox of high utility and low exchangeability. This distinction begged questions rather than solved them and for another hundred years economists sought for a satisfactory formulation. Finally, toward the end of the last century—though it is now recognized that their work had been extensively anticipated—the three economists of marginal utility (Karl Menger, an Austrian; William Stanley Jevons, an Englishman; and John Bates Clark, an American) produced more or less simultaneously the explanation which in broad substance still serves. The urgency of desire is a function of the quantity of goods which the individual has available to satisfy that desire. The larger the stock the less the satisfactions from an increment. And the less, also, the willingness to pay. Since diamonds for most people are

2. The provenance of the theory of consumer behavior is sketched in Mr. I. D. M. Little's interesting article "A Reformulation of Consumer Behavior," *Oxford Economic Papers*, New Series, vol. 1, no. 1 (January 1949), p. 99.
3. *Wealth of Nations*. Smith did not foresee the industrial diamond.

in comparatively meager supply, the satisfaction from an additional one is great, and the potential willingness to pay is likewise high. The case of water is just the reverse. It also follows that where the supply of a good can be readily increased at low cost, its value in exchange will reflect that ease of reproduction and the low urgency of the marginal desires it thus comes to satisfy. This will be so no matter how difficult it may be (as with water) to dispense entirely with the item in question.

The doctrine of diminishing marginal utility, as it was enshrined in the economics textbooks, seemed to put economic ideas squarely on the side of the diminishing importance of production under conditions of increasing affluence. With increasing per capita real income, men are able to satisfy additional wants. These are of a lower order of urgency. This being so, the production that provides the goods that satisfy these less urgent wants must also be of smaller (and declining) importance. In Ricardo's England the supply of bread for many was meager. The satisfaction resulting from an increment in the bread supply —from a higher money income, bread prices being the same, or the same money income, bread prices being lower—was great. Hunger was lessened; life itself might be extended. Certainly any measure to increase the bread supply merited the deep and serious interest of the public-spirited citizen.

In the contemporary United States the supply of bread is plentiful and the supply of bread grains even redundant. The yield of satisfactions from a marginal increment in the wheat supply is small. To a Secretary of Agriculture it is indubitably negative. Measures to increase the wheat supply are not, therefore, a socially urgent preoccupation of publicly concerned citizens. These are more likely to be found spending their time devising schemes for the effective control of wheat production. And having extended their bread consumption to the point where its marginal utility is very low, people have gone on to spend their income on other things. Since these other goods entered their consumption pattern after bread, there is a presumption that they are not very urgent either—that *their* consumption has been carried, as with wheat, to the point where marginal utility is small or even negligible. So it must be assumed that the importance of marginal increments of all production is low and declining. The effect of increasing affluence is to minimize the importance of economic goals. Production and productivity become less and less important.

The concept of diminishing marginal utility was, and remains, one of the indispensable ideas of economics. Since it conceded so much to the notion of diminishing urgency of wants, and hence of production, it was remarkable indeed that the situation was retrieved. This was done—and brilliantly. The diminishing urgency of wants was not admitted. In part this was accomplished in the name of refined scientific method which, as so often at the higher levels of sophistication, proved a formidable bulwark of the conventional wisdom. Obvious but inconvenient evidence was rejected on the grounds that it could not be scientifically assimilated. But even beyond this, it has been necessary at times simply to close one's eyes to phenomena which could not be reconciled with convenience.

Economics took general cognizance of the fact that an almost infinite variety of goods await the consumer's attention. At the more elementary (and also the more subjective) levels of economic analysis it is assumed that, while the marginal utility of the individual good declines in accordance with the indubitable law, the utility or satisfaction from new and different kinds of goods does not diminish appreciably. So long as the consumer adds new products—seeks variety rather than quantity—he may, like a museum, accumulate without diminishing the urgency of his wants. Since even in Los Angeles the average consumer owns only a fraction of the different kinds of goods he might conceivably possess, there is all but unlimited opportunity for adding such products. The rewards to the possessors are more or less proportional to the supply. The production that supplies these goods and services, since it renders undiminished utility, remains of undiminished importance.

This position ignores the obvious fact that some things are acquired before others and that, presumably, the more important things come first. This, as observed previously, implies a declining urgency of need. However, in the slightly more sophisticated theory this conclusion is rejected. The rejection centers on the denial that anything very useful can be said of the comparative states of mind and satisfaction of the consumer at different periods of time. Few students of economics, even in the elementary course, now escape without a warning against the error of intertemporal comparisons of the utility from given acts of consumption. Yesterday the man with a minimal but increasing real income was reaping the satisfactions which came from a decent diet and a roof that no longer leaked water on his face. Today, after a large increase in his income, he has extended his consumption to include suede shoes and a weekly visit to the races. But to say that his satisfactions from these latter amenities and recreations are less than from the additional calories and the freedom from rain is wholly improper. Things have changed; he is a different man; there is no real standard for comparison. That, as of a given time, an individual will derive lesser satisfactions from the marginal increments to a given stock of goods, and accordingly cannot be induced to pay as much for them, is conceded. But this tells us nothing of the satisfactions from such additional goods, and more particularly from different goods, when they are acquired at a later time. The conclusion follows. One cannot be sure that the satisfaction from these temporally later increases in the individual's stock of goods diminishes. Hence one cannot suggest that the production which supplies it is of diminishing urgency.

A moment's reflection on what has been accomplished will be worth while. The notion of diminishing utility still serves its indispensable purpose of relating urgency of desire and consequent willingness to pay to quantity. At any given time the more the individual might have, the less would be the satisfaction he would derive from additions to his stock and the less he would be willing to pay. The reactions of the community will be the aggregate of the reactions of the individuals it comprises. Hence the greater the supply the less the willingness to pay for marginal increments and hence the demand curve familiar to all who have made even the most modest venture into economic theory. But, at the same time, the question of the diminishing urgency of consumption is elided. For, while the question of willingness to pay for additional quantities is based on a hypothesis as to behavior in face of these quantities at a given point of time, an increase in stock of consumers' goods, as the result of an increase in real income, can occur only over time. On the yield of satisfactions from this the economist has nothing to say. In the name of good scientific method he is prevented from saying anything. There is room, however, for the broad assumption—given the large and ever-growing variety of goods awaiting the consumer's attention—that wants have a sustained urgency. In any case, it can safely be concluded that more goods will satisfy more wants than fewer goods. And the assumption that goods are an important and even an urgent thing to provide stalks unchallenged behind, for have not goods always been important for relieving the privation of mankind? It will be evident that economics has brilliantly retrieved the dangers to itself and to its goals that were inherent in diminishing marginal utility.

There has been dissent. Keynes observed that the needs of human beings "fall into two classes—those needs which are absolute in the sense that we feel them whatever the situation of our fellow human beings may be, and those which are relative only in that their satisfaction lifts us above, makes us feel superior to, our fellows." While conceding that the second class of wants might be insatiable, he argued that the first were capable of being satisfied and went on to conclude that "assuming no important wars and no important increase in population the *economic problem* may be solved, or at least within sight of solution, within a hundred years. This means the economic problem is not—if we look into the future—*the permanent problem of the human race*." [4] However, on this conclusion Keynes made no headway. In contending with the conventional wisdom he, no less than others, needed the support of circumstance. And in contrast with his remedy for depressions this he did not yet have.

THE DEPENDENCE EFFECT

The notion that wants do not become less urgent the more amply the individual is supplied is broadly repugnant to common sense. It is something to be believed only by those who wish to believe. Yet the conventional wisdom must be tackled on its own terrain. Intertemporal comparisons of an individual's state of mind do rest on doubtful grounds. Who can say for sure that the deprivation which afflicts him with hunger is more painful than the deprivation which afflicts him with envy of his neighbor's new car? In the time that has passed since he was poor his soul may have become subject to a new and deeper searing.

4. J. M. Keynes, *Essays in Persuasion*, "Economic Possibilities for Our Grandchildren," pp. 365–66. The italics are in the original. Notice that Keynes, as always little bound by the conventional rules, did not hesitate to commit the unpardonable sin of distinguishing between categories of desire.

And where a society is concerned, comparisons between marginal satisfactions when it is poor and those when it is affluent will involve not only the same individual at different times but different individuals at different times. The scholar who wishes to believe that with increasing affluence there is no reduction in the urgency of desires and goods is not without points for debate. However plausible the case against him, it cannot be proven. In the defense of the conventional wisdom this amounts almost to invulnerability.

However, there is a flaw in the case. If the individual's wants are to be urgent they must be original with himself. They cannot be urgent if they must be contrived for him. And above all they must not be contrived by the process of production by which they are satisfied. For this means that the whole case for the urgency of production, based on the urgency of wants, falls to the ground. One cannot defend production as satisfying wants if that production creates the wants.

Were it so that a man on arising each morning was assailed by demons which instilled in him a passion sometimes for silk shirts, sometimes for kitchenware, sometimes for chamber pots, and sometimes for orange squash, there would be every reason to applaud the effort to find the goods, however odd, that quenched this flame. But should it be that his passion was the result of his first having cultivated the demons, and should it also be that his effort to allay it stirred the demons to ever greater and greater effort, there would be question as to how rational was his solution. Unless restrained by conventional attitudes, he might wonder if the solution lay with more goods or fewer demons.

So it is that if production creates the wants it seeks to satisfy, or if the wants emerge *pari passu* with the production, then the urgency of the wants can no longer be used to defend the urgency of the production. Production only fills a void that it has itself created.

The point is so central that it must be pressed. Consumer wants can have bizarre, frivolous, or even immoral origins, and an admirable case can still be made for a society that seeks to satisfy them. But the case cannot stand if it is the process of satisfying wants that creates the wants. For then the individual who urges the importance of production to satisfy these wants is precisely in the position of the onlooker who applauds the efforts of the squirrel to keep abreast of the wheel that is propelled by his own efforts.

That wants are, in fact, the fruit of production will now be denied by few serious scholars. And a considerable number of economists, though not always in full knowledge of the implications, have conceded the point. In the observation cited earlier Keynes noted that needs of "the second class," i.e., those that are the result of efforts to keep abreast or ahead of one's fellow being "may indeed be insatiable; for the higher the general level the higher still are they." [5] And emulation has always played a considerable role in the views of other economists of want creation. One man's consumption becomes his neighbor's wish. This already means that the process by which wants are satisfied is also the process by which wants are created. The more wants that are satisfied the more new ones are born.

However, the argument has been carried farther. A leading modern theorist of consumer behavior, Professor Duesenberry, has stated explicitly that "ours is a society in which one of the principal social goals is a higher standard of living. . . . [This] has great significance for the theory of consumption . . . the desire to get superior goods takes on a life of its own. It provides a drive to higher expenditure which may even be stronger than that arising out of the needs which are supposed to be satisfied by that expenditure." [6] The implications of this view are impressive. The notion of independently established need now sinks into the background. Because the society sets great store by ability to produce a high living standard, it evaluates people by the products they possess. The urge to consume is fathered by the value system which emphasizes the ability of the society to produce. The more that is produced the more that must be owned in order to maintain the appropriate prestige. The latter is an important point, for, without going as far as Duesenberry in reducing goods to the role of symbols of prestige in the affluent society, it is plain that his argument fully implies that the production of goods creates the wants that the goods are presumed to satisfy.

The even more direct link between production and wants is provided by the institutions of modern advertising and salesman-

5. *Op. cit.*
6. James S. Duesenberry, *Income, Saving and the Theory of Consumer Behavior* (Cambridge, Mass.: Harvard University Press, 1949), p. 28.

ship. These cannot be reconciled with the notion of independently determined desires, for their central function is to create desires —to bring into being wants that previously did not exist. This is accomplished by the producer of the goods or at his behest. A broad empirical relationship exists between what is spent on production of consumers' goods and what is spent in synthesizing the desires for that production. A new consumer product must be introduced with a suitable advertising campaign to arouse an interest in it. The path for an expansion of output must be paved by a suitable expansion in the advertising budget. Outlays for the manufacturing of a product are not more important in the strategy of modern business enterprise than outlays for the manufacturing of demand for the product. None of this is novel. All would be regarded as elementary by the most retarded student in the nation's most primitive school of business administration. The cost of this want formation is formidable. In 1956 total advertising expenditure—though, as noted, not all of it may be assigned to the synthesis of wants—amounted to about ten billion dollars. For some years it had been increasing at a rate in excess of a billion dollars a year. Obviously, such outlays must be integrated with the theory of consumer demand. They are too big to be ignored.

But such integration means recognizing that wants are dependent on production. It accords to the producer the function both of making the goods and of making the desires for them. It recognizes that production, not only passively through emulation, but actively through advertising and related activities, creates the wants it seeks to satisfy.

The businessman and the lay reader will be puzzled over the emphasis which I give to a seemingly obvious point. The point is indeed obvious. But it is one which, to a singular degree, economists have resisted. They have sensed, as the layman does not, the damage to established ideas which lurks in these relationships. As a result, incredibly, they have closed their eyes (and ears) to the most obtrusive of all economic phenomena, namely modern want creation.

This is not to say that the evidence affirming the dependence of wants on advertising has been entirely ignored. It is one reason why advertising has so long been regarded with such uneasiness by economists. Here is something which cannot be accommodated easily to existing theory. More pervious scholars have speculated on the urgency of desires which are so obviously the fruit of such expensively contrived campaigns for popular attention. Is a new breakfast cereal or detergent so much wanted if so much must be spent to compel in the consumer the sense of want? But there has been little tendency to go on to examine the implications of this for the theory of consumer demand and even less for the importance of production and productive efficiency. These have remained sacrosanct. More often the uneasiness has been manifested in a general disapproval of advertising and advertising men, leading to the occasional suggestion that they shouldn't exist. Such suggestions have usually been ill received.

And so the notion of independently determined wants still survives. In the face of all the forces of modern salesmanship it still rules, almost undefiled, in the textbooks. And it still remains the economist's mission—and on few matters is the pedagogy so firm—to seek unquestioningly the means for filling these wants. This being so, production remains of prime urgency. We have here, perhaps, the ultimate triumph of the conventional wisdom in its resistance to the evidence of the eyes. To equal it one must imagine a humanitarian who was long ago persuaded of the grievous shortage of hospital facilities in the town. He continues to importune the passers-by for money for more beds and refuses to notice that the town doctor is deftly knocking over pedestrians with his car to keep up the occupancy.

And in unraveling the complex we should always be careful not to overlook the obvious. The fact that wants can be synthesized by advertising, catalyzed by salesmanship, and shaped by the discreet manipulations of the persuaders shows that they are not very urgent. A man who is hungry need never be told of his need for food. If he is inspired by his appetite, he is immune to the influence of Messrs. Batten, Barton, Durstine & Osborn. The latter are effective only with those who are so far removed from physical want that they do not already know what they want. In this state alone men are open to persuasion.

The general conclusion of these pages is of such importance for this essay that it had perhaps best be put with some formality. As a society becomes increasingly affluent, wants are increasingly created by the process by which they are satisfied. This may operate passively. Increases in consumption, the counterpart of increases in production, act by suggestion or emulation to create wants. Or producers may proceed actively to create wants through advertising and salesmanship. Wants thus come to depend on output. In technical terms it can no longer be assumed that welfare is greater at an all-round higher level of production than at a lower one. It may be the same. The higher level of production has, merely, a higher level of want creation necessitating a higher level of want satisfaction. There will be frequent occasion to refer to the way wants depend on the process by which they are satisfied. It will be convenient to call it the Dependence Effect.

We may now contemplate briefly the conclusions to which this analysis has brought us.

Plainly the theory of consumer demand is a peculiarly treacherous friend of the present goals of economics. At first glance it seems to defend the continuing urgency of production and our preoccupation with it as a goal. The economist does not enter into the dubious moral arguments about the importance or virtue of the wants to be satisfied. He doesn't pretend to compare mental states of the same or different people at different times and to suggest that one is less urgent than another. The desire is there. That for him is sufficient. He sets about in a workmanlike way to satisfy desire, and accordingly he sets the proper store by the production that does. Like woman's his work is never done.

But this rationalization, handsomely though it seems to serve, turns destructively on those who advance it once it is conceded that wants are themselves both passively and deliberately the fruits of the process by which they are satisfied. Then the production of goods satisfies the wants that the consumption of these goods creates or that the producers of goods synthesize. Production induces more wants and the need for more production. So far, in a major *tour de force*, the implications have been ignored. But this obviously is a perilous solution. It cannot long survive discussion.

Among the many models of the good society no one has urged the squirrel wheel. Moreover, the wheel is not one that revolves with perfect smoothness. Aside from its dubious cultural charm, there are serious structural weaknesses which may one day embarrass us. For the moment, however, it is sufficient to reflect on the difficult terrain which we are traversing. We find our concern for goods undermined. It does not arise in spontaneous consumer need. Rather, the dependence effect means that it grows out of the process of production itself. If production is to increase, the wants must be effectively contrived. In the absence of the contrivance the increase would not occur. This is not true of all goods, but that it is true of a substantial part is sufficient. It means that since the demand for this part would not exist, were it not contrived, its utility or urgency, ex contrivance, is zero. If we regard this production as marginal, we may say that the marginal utility of present aggregate output, ex advertising and salesmanship, is zero. Clearly the attitudes and values which make production the central achievement of our society have some exceptionally twisted roots. . . .

THE THEORY OF SOCIAL BALANCE

The final problem of the productive society is what it produces. This manifests itself in an implacable tendency to provide an opulent supply of some things and a niggardly yield of others. This disparity carries to the point where it is a cause of social discomfort and social unhealth. The line which divides our area of wealth from our area of poverty is roughly that which divides privately produced and marketed goods and services from publicly rendered services. Our wealth in the first is not only in startling contrast with the meagerness of the latter, but our wealth in privately produced goods is, to a marked degree, the cause of crisis in the supply of public services. For we have failed to see the importance, indeed the urgent need, of maintaining a balance between the two.

This disparity between our flow of private and public goods and services is no matter of subjective judgment. On the contrary, it is the source of the most extensive comment which only stops short of the direct contrast being made here. In the years following World War II, the papers of any major city—those of New York were an excellent example—told daily of the shortages and shortcomings in the elementary municipal and metropolitan services. The schools were old and overcrowded. The police force was under strength and underpaid. The parks and playgrounds were insufficient. Streets and empty lots were filthy, and the sanitation staff was underequipped and in need of men. Access to the city by those who work there was uncertain and painful and becoming more so. Internal transportation was overcrowded, unhealthful, and dirty. So was the air. Parking on the streets had to be prohibited, and there was no space elsewhere. These deficiencies were not in new and novel services but in old and established ones. Cities have long swept their streets, helped their people move around, educated them, kept order, and provided horse rails for vehicles which sought to pause. That their residents should have a nontoxic supply of air suggests no revolutionary dalliance with socialism.

The discussion of this public poverty competed, on the whole successfully, with the stories of ever-increasing opulence in privately produced goods. The Gross National Product was rising. So were retail sales. So was personal income. Labor productivity had also advanced. The automobiles that could not be parked were being produced at an expanded rate. The children, though without schools, subject in the playgrounds to the affectionate interest of adults with odd tastes, and disposed to increasingly imaginative forms of delinquency, were admirably equipped with television sets. We had difficulty finding storage space for the great surpluses of food despite a national disposition to obesity. Food was grown and packaged under private auspices. The care and refreshment of the mind, in contrast with the stomach, was principally in the public domain. Our colleges and universities were severely overcrowded and underprovided, and the same was true of the mental hospitals.

The contrast was and remains evident not alone to those who read. The family which takes its mauve and cerise, air-conditioned, power-steered, and power-braked automobile out for a tour passes through cities that are badly paved, made hideous by litter, blighted buildings, billboards, and posts for wires that should long since have been put underground. They pass on into a countryside that has been rendered largely invisible by commercial art. (The goods which the latter advertises have an absolute priority in our value system. Such aesthetic considerations as a view of the countryside accordingly come second. On such matters we are consistent.) They picnic on exquisitely packaged food from a portable icebox by a polluted stream and go on to spend the night at a park which is a menace to public health and morals. Just before dozing off on an air mattress, beneath a nylon tent, amid the stench of decaying refuse, they may reflect vaguely on the curious unevenness of their blessings. Is this, indeed, the American genius?

In the production of goods within the private economy it has long been recognized that a tolerably close relationship must be maintained between the production of various kinds of products. Just as there must be balance in what a community produces, so there must also be balance in what the community consumes. An increase in the use of one product creates, ineluctably, a requirement for others. If we are to consume more automobiles, we must have more gasoline. There must be more insurance as well as more space on which to operate them. Beyond a certain point more and better food appears to mean increased need for medical services. This is the certain result of the increased consumption of tobacco and alcohol. More vacations require more hotels and more fishing rods. And so forth. With rare exceptions—shortages of doctors are an exception which suggests the rule—this balance is also maintained quite effortlessly so far as goods for private sale and consumption are concerned. The price system plus a rounded condition of opulence is again the agency.

However, the relationships we are here discussing are not confined to the private economy. They operate comprehensively over the whole span of private and public services. As surely as an increase in the output of automobiles puts new demands on the steel industry so, also, it places new demands on public services. Similarly, every increase in the consumption of private goods will normally mean some facilitating or protective step by the state. In all cases if these services are not forthcoming, the consequences will be in some degree ill. It will be convenient to have a term which suggests a satisfactory relationship between the supply of privately produced goods and services and those of the state, and we may call it social balance.

The problem of social balance is ubiquitous, and frequently it is obtrusive. As noted, an increase in the consumption of automobiles requires a facilitating supply of streets, highways, traffic control, and parking space. The protective services of the police and the highway patrols must also be available, as must those of the hospitals. Although the need for balance here is extraordinarily clear, our use of privately produced vehicles has, on occasion, got far out of line with the supply of the related public services. The result has been hideous road congestion, an annual massacre of impressive proportions, and chronic colitis in the cities. As on the ground, so also in the air. Planes collide with disquieting consequences for those within when the public provision for air traffic control fails to keep pace with private use of the airways.

But the auto and the airplane, versus the space to use them, are merely an exceptionally visible example of a requirement that is pervasive. The more goods people procure, the more packages they discard and the more trash that must be carried away. If the appropriate sanitation services are not provided, the counterpart of increasing opulence will be deepening filth. The greater the wealth the thicker will be the dirt. This indubitably describes a tendency of our time. As more goods are produced and owned, the greater are the opportunities for fraud and the more property that must be protected. If the provision of public law enforcement services does not keep pace, the counterpart of increased well-being will, we may be certain, be increased crime.

The city of Los Angeles, in modern times, is a near-classic study in the problem of social balance. Magnificently efficient factories and oil refineries, a lavish supply of automobiles, a vast consumption of handsomely packaged products, coupled with the absence of a municipal trash collection service which forced the use of home incinerators, made the air nearly unbreathable for an appreciable part of each year. Air pollution could be controlled only by a complex and highly developed set of public services—by better knowledge stemming from more research, better policing, a municipal trash collection service, and possibly the assertion of the priority of clean air over the production of goods. These were long in coming. The agony of a city without usable air was the result. . . .

The case for social balance has, so far, been put negatively. Failure to keep public services in minimal relation to private production and use of goods is a cause of social disorder or impairs economic performance. The matter may now be put affirmatively. By failing to exploit the opportunity to expand public production we are missing opportunities for enjoyment which otherwise we might have had. Presumably a community can be as well rewarded by buying better schools or better parks as by buying bigger automobiles. By concentrating on the latter rather than the former it is failing to maximize its satisfactions. As with schools in the community, so with public services over the country at large. It is scarcely sensible that we should satisfy our wants in private goods with reckless abundance, while in the case of public goods, on the evidence of the eye, we practice extreme self-denial. So, far from systematically exploiting the opportunities to derive use and pleasure from these services, we do not supply what would keep us out of trouble.

The conventional wisdom holds that the community, large or small, makes a decision as to how much it will devote to its public services. This decision is arrived at by democratic process. Subject to the imperfections and uncertainties of democracy, people decide how much of their private income and goods they will surrender in order to have public services of which they are in greater need. Thus there is a balance, however rough, in the enjoyments to be had from private goods and services and those rendered by public authority.

It will be obvious, however, that this view depends on the notion of independently determined consumer wants. In such a world one could with some reason defend the doctrine that the consumer, as a voter, makes an independent choice between public and private goods. But given the dependence effect—given that consumer wants are created by the process by which they are satisfied—the consumer makes no such choice. He is subject to the forces of advertising and emulation by which production creates its own demand. Advertising operates exclusively, and emulation mainly, on behalf of privately produced goods and services.[7] Since management and emulative effects operate on behalf of private production, public services will have an inherent tendency to lag behind. Automobile demand which is expensively synthesized will inevitably have a much larger claim on income than parks or public health or even roads where no such influence operates. The engines of mass communication, in their highest state of development, assail the eyes and ears of the community on behalf of more beer but not of more schools. Even in the conventional wisdom it will scarcely be contended that this leads to an equal choice between the two.

7. Emulation does operate between communities. A new school or a new highway in one community does exert pressure on others to remain abreast. However, as compared with the pervasive effects of emulation in extending the demand for privately produced consumer's goods there will be agreement, I think, that this intercommunity effect is probably small.

The competition is especially unequal for new products and services. Every corner of the public psyche is canvassed by some of the nation's most talented citizens to see if the desire for some merchantable product can be cultivated. No similar process operates on behalf of the nonmerchantable services of the state. Indeed, while we take the cultivation of new private wants for granted we would be measurably shocked to see it applied to public services. The scientist or engineer or advertising man who devotes himself to developing a new carburetor, cleanser, or depilatory for which the public recognizes no need and will feel none until an advertising campaign arouses it, is one of the valued members of our society. A politician or a public servant who dreams up a new public service is a wastrel. Few public offenses are more reprehensible.

So much for the influences which operate on the decision between public and private production. The calm decision between public and private consumption pictured by the conventional wisdom is, in fact, a remarkable example of the error which arises from viewing social behavior out of context. The inherent tendency will always be for public services to fall behind private production. . . .

THE REDRESS OF BALANCE

Our next task is to find a way of obtaining and then of maintaining a balance in the great flow of goods and services with which our wealth each year rewards us. In particular, we must find a way to remedy the poverty which afflicts us in public services and which is in such increasingly bizarre contrast with our affluence in private goods.

The problem will not be settled by a resolve to spend more for schools and streets and other services and to tax accordingly. Such decisions are made every day, and they do not come to grips with the causes of the imbalance. These lie much deeper. The most important difference between private and public goods and services is a technical one. The first lend themselves to being sold to individuals. The second do not. In the evolution of economic enterprise, the things which could be produced and sold for a price were taken over by private producers. Those that could not, but which were in the end no less urgent for that reason, remained with the state. Bread and steel went naturally to private enterprise, for they could readily be produced and marketed by individuals to individuals. Police protection, sanitation, and sewer systems remained with public authority for, on the whole, they could not. Once the decision was taken to make education universal and compulsory, it ceased to be a marketable commodity. With the rise of the national state so did national defense. The line between public and private activity, as we view it at any given moment, is the product of many forces—tradition, ideological preference, and social urgency all play some part. But to a far greater degree than is commonly supposed, functions accrue to the state because, as a purely technical matter, there is no alternative to public management.

The goods and services which are marketable at a price have a position of elementary strategic advantage in the economy. Their price provides the income which commands labor, capital, and raw materials for production. This is inherent in the productive process. In the absence of social intervention, private production will monopolize all resources. Only as something is done about it will resources become available for public services.

The solution is a system of taxation which automatically makes a pro rata share of increasing income available to public authority for public purposes. The task of public authority, like that of private individuals, will be to distribute this increase in accordance with relative need. Schools and roads will then no longer be at a disadvantage as compared with automobiles and television sets in having to prove absolute justification.

However, even though the higher urgency of the services for social balance is conceded, there is still the problem of providing the revenue. And since it is income taxes that must be used, the question of social balance can easily be lost sight of in the reopened argument over equality. The truce will be broken and liberals and conservatives will join battle on this issue and forget about the poverty in the public services that awaits correction and the poverty of people which can only be corrected at increased public cost. All this—schools, hospitals, even the scientific research on which increased production depends—must wait while we debate the ancient and unresolvable question of whether the rich are too rich.

The only hope—and in the nature of things it rests primarily with liberals—is to separate the issue of equality from that of social balance. The second is by far the more important question.

The rational liberal, in the future, will resist tax reduction, even that which ostensibly favors the poor, if it is at the price of social balance. . . .

One final observation may be made. There will be question as to what is the test of balance—at what point may we conclude that balance has been achieved in the satisfaction of private and public needs. The answer is that no test can be applied, for none exists. The traditional formulation is that the satisfaction returned to the community from a marginal increment of resources devoted to public purposes should be equal to the satisfaction of the same increment in private employment. These are incommensurate, partly because different people are involved, and partly because it makes the cardinal error of comparing satisfaction of wants that are synthesized with those that are not.

But a precise equilibrium is not very important. For another mark of an affluent society is the opportunity for the existence of a considerable margin for error on such matters. The present imbalance is clear, as are the forces and ideas which give the priority to private as compared with public goods. This being so, the direction in which we move to correct matters is utterly plain. We can also assume, given the power of the forces that have operated to accord a priority to private goods, that the distance to be traversed is considerable. When we arrive, the opulence of our private consumption will no longer be in contrast with the poverty of our schools, the unloveliness and congestion of our cities, our inability to get to work without struggle, and the social disorder that is associated with imbalance. But the precise point of balance will never be defined. This will be of comfort only to those who believe that any failure of definition can be made to score decisively against a larger idea.

The *Non Sequitur* of the "Dependence Effect"

F. A. HAYEK

Friedrich A. Hayek is Professor of Economics at the University of Freiburg. In such books as The Road to Serfdom *and* The Constitution of Liberty *he examines the economic and political conditions for a free society.*

FOR WELL over a hundred years the critics of the free enterprise system have resorted to the argument that if production were only organized rationally, there would be no economic problem. Rather than face the problem which scarcity creates, socialist reformers have tended to deny that scarcity existed. Ever since the Saint-Simonians their contention has been that the problem of production has been solved and only the problem of distribution remains. However absurd this contention must appear to us with respect to the time when it was first advanced, it still has some persuasive power when repeated with reference to the present.

The latest form of this old contention is expounded in *The Affluent Society* by Professor J. K. Galbraith. He attempts to demonstrate that in our affluent society the important private needs are already satisfied and the urgent need is therefore no longer a further expansion of the output of commodities but an increase of those services which are supplied (and presumably can be supplied only) by government. Though this book has been extensively discussed since its publication in 1958, its central thesis still requires some further examination.

I believe the author would agree that his argument turns upon the "Dependence Effect" explained in [the article which precedes this one]. The argument starts from the assertion that a great part of the wants which are still unsatisfied in modern society are not wants which would be experienced spontaneously by the individual if left to himself, but are wants which are created by

45

the process by which they are satisfied. It is then represented as self-evident that for this reason such wants cannot be urgent or important. This crucial conclusion appears to be a complete *non sequitur* and it would seem that with it the whole argument of the book collapses.

The first part of the argument is of course perfectly true: we would not desire any of the amenities of civilization—or even of the most primitive culture—if we did not live in a society in which others provide them. The innate wants are probably confined to food, shelter, and sex. All the rest we learn to desire because we see others enjoying various things. To say that a desire is not important because it is not innate is to say that the whole cultural achievement of man is not important.

The cultural origin of practically all the needs of civilized life must of course not be confused with the fact that there are some desires which aim, not at a satisfaction derived directly from the use of an object, but only from the status which its consumption is expected to confer. In a passage which Professor Galbraith quotes, Lord Keynes seems to treat the latter sort of Veblenesque conspicuous consumption [1] as the only alternative "to those needs which are absolute in the sense that we feel them whatever the situation of our fellow human beings may be." If the latter phrase is interpreted to exclude all the needs for goods which are felt only because these goods are known to be produced, these two Keynesian classes describe of course only extreme types of wants, but disregard the overwhelming majority of goods on which civilized life rests. Very few needs indeed are "absolute" in the sense that they are independent of social environment or of the

---

1. [Hayek is referring here to Thorstein Veblen (1857–1929), the American economist and social critic, who maintained that the "conspicuous consumption of valuable goods" was the principal means by which social standing could be enhanced. "The quasi-peaceable gentleman of leisure not only consumes of the staff of life but his consumption undergoes a specialization as regards the quality of goods consumed. He consumes freely, and of the best, in food, drink, narcotics, shelter, services, ornaments, apparel, weapons, and accoutrements, amusements, amulets, and idols of divinities. . . . Since the consumption of these more excellent goods is an evidence of wealth, it becomes honorific; and conversely the failure to consume in due quantity and quality becomes a mark of inferiority and demerit" (*The Theory of the Leisure Class,* Modern Library Edition, 1934, pp. 73–74). *Editor.*]

example of others, and that their satisfaction is an indispensable condition for the preservation of the individual or of the species. Most needs which make us act are needs for things which only civilization teaches us exist at all, and these things are wanted by us because they produce feelings or emotions which we would not know if it were not for our cultural inheritance. Are not in this sense probably all our esthetic feelings "acquired tastes"?

How complete a *non sequitur* Professor Galbraith's conclusion represents is seen most clearly if we apply the argument to any product of the arts, be it music, painting, or literature. If the fact that people would not feel the need for something if it were not produced did prove that such products are of small value, all those highest products of human endeavor would be of small value. Professor Galbraith's argument could be easily employed, without any change of the essential terms, to demonstrate the worthlessness of literature or any other form of art. Surely an individual's want for literature is not original with himself in the sense that he would experience it if literature were not produced. Does this then mean that the production of literature cannot be defended as satisfying a want because it is only the production which provokes the demand? In this, as in the case of all cultural needs, it is unquestionably, in Professor Galbraith's words, "the process of satisfying the wants that creates the wants." There have never been "independently determined desires for" literature before literature has been produced and books certainly do not serve the "simple mode of enjoyment which requires no previous conditioning of the consumer." Clearly my taste for the novels of Jane Austen or Anthony Trollope or C. P. Snow is not "original with myself." But is it not rather absurd to conclude from this that it is less important than, say, the need for education? Public education indeed seems to regard it as one of its tasks to instill a taste for literature in the young and even employs producers of literature for that purpose. Is this want creation by the producer reprehensible? Or does the fact that some of the pupils may possess a taste for poetry only because of the efforts of their teachers prove that since "it does not arise in spontaneous consumer need and the demand would not exist were it not contrived, its utility or urgency, ex contrivance, is zero"?

The appearance that the conclusions follow from the admitted

facts is made possible by an obscurity of the wording of the argument with respect to which it is difficult to know whether the
author is himself the victim of a confusion or whether he skilfully
uses ambiguous terms to make the conclusion appear plausible.
The obscurity concerns the implied assertion that the wants of
consumers are determined by the producers. Professor Galbraith
avoids in this connection any terms as crude and definite as
"determine." The expressions he employs, such as that wants are
"dependent on" or the "fruits of" production, or that "production
creates the wants" do, of course, suggest determination but avoid
saying so in plain terms. After what has already been said it is
of course obvious that the knowledge of what is being produced
is one of the many factors on which depends what people will
want. It would scarcely be an exaggeration to say that contemporary man, in all fields where he has not yet formed firm habits,
tends to find out what he wants by looking at what his neighbours
do and at various displays of goods (physical or in catalogues or
advertisements) and then choosing what he likes best.

In this sense the tastes of man, as is also true of his opinions
and beliefs and indeed much of his personality, are shaped in a
great measure by his cultural environment. But though in some
contexts it would perhaps be legitimate to express this by a phrase
like "production creates the wants," the circumstances mentioned
would clearly not justify the contention that particular producers
can deliberately determine the wants of particular consumers.
The efforts of all producers will certainly be directed towards
that end; but how far any individual producer will succeed will
depend not only on what he does but also on what the others do
and on a great many other influences operating upon the consumer. The joint but unco-ordinated efforts of the producers
merely create one element of the environment by which the wants
of the consumers are shaped. It is because each individual producer thinks that the consumers can be persuaded to like his
products that he endeavours to influence them. But though this
effort is part of the influences which shape consumers' tastes,
no producer can in any real sense "determine" them. This, however, is clearly implied in such statements as that wants are "both
passively and deliberately the fruits of the process by which
they are satisfied." If the producer could in fact deliberately

determine what the consumers will want, Professor Galbraith's conclusions would have some validity. But though this is skilfully suggested, it is nowhere made credible, and could hardly be made credible because it is not true. Though the range of choice open to the consumers is the joint result of, among other things, the efforts of all producers who vie with each other in making their respective products appear more attractive than those of their competitors, every particular consumer still has the choice between all those different offers.

A fuller examination of this process would, of course, have to consider how, after the efforts of some producers have actually swayed some consumers, it becomes the example of the various consumers thus persuaded which will influence the remaining consumers. This can be mentioned here only to emphasize that even if each consumer were exposed to pressure of only one producer, the harmful effects which are apprehended from this would soon be offset by the much more powerful example of his fellows. It is of course fashionable to treat this influence of the example of others (or, what comes to the same thing, the learning from the experience made by others) as if it all amounted to an attempt at keeping up with the Joneses and for that reason was to be regarded as detrimental. It seems to me not only that the importance of this factor is usually greatly exaggerated but also that it is not really relevant to Professor Galbraith's main thesis. But it might be worthwhile briefly to ask what, assuming that some expenditure were actually determined solely by a desire of keeping up with the Joneses, that would really prove?

At least in Europe we used to be familiar with a type of persons who often denied themselves even enough food in order to maintain an appearance of respectability or gentility in dress and style of life. We may regard this as a misguided effort, but surely it would not prove that the income of such persons was larger than they knew how to use wisely. That the appearance of success, or wealth, may to some people seem more important than many other needs, does in no way prove that the needs they sacrifice to the former are unimportant. In the same way, even though people are often persuaded to spend unwisely, this surely is no evidence that they do not still have important unsatisfied needs.

Professor Galbraith's attempt to give an apparent scientific proof for the contention that the need for the production of more commodities has greatly decreased seems to me to have broken down completely. With it goes the claim to have produced a valid argument which justifies the use of coercion to make people employ their income for those purposes of which he approves. It is not to be denied that there is some originality in this latest version of the old socialist argument. For over a hundred years we have been exhorted to embrace socialism because it would give us more goods. Since it has so lamentably failed to achieve this where it has been tried, we are now urged to adopt it because more goods after all are not important. The aim is still progressively to increase the share of the resources whose use is determined by political authority and the coercion of any dissenting minority. It is not surprising, therefore, that Professor Galbraith's thesis has been most enthusiastically received by the intellectuals of the British Labour Party where his influence bids fair to displace that of the late Lord Keynes. It is more curious that in this country it is not recognized as an outright socialist argument and often seems to appeal to people on the opposite end of the political spectrum. But this is probably only another instance of the familiar fact that on these matters the extremes frequently meet.

Public versus Private: Could Galbraith Be Wrong?

HENRY C. WALLICH

Henry C. Wallich is Professor of Economics at Yale University. His book The Cost of Freedom, *from which a part of this essay is taken, argues that we must not ask maximum efficiency of our economic system if we also value individual freedom.*

IN ADDITION to free advice about growth, the nation has received helpful suggestions of another sort, in a rather opposite vein. It has been argued that we have all the production we need and to spare, but that too much of our growth has gone into private consumption, too little into public. We are said to be wasting our substance on trivia while allowing urgent public needs to go uncared for. This view does not complain of inadequate growth. But it sees us riding in tail-finned, oversized automobiles through cities that are becoming slums, finds our children sitting glued to the latest TV models but lacking schools where they can learn to read properly, and generally charges us with putting private profligacy ahead of public provision.

The general doctrine that in the United States public needs tend to be underfinanced in relation to private I first heard many years ago from my old teacher Alvin Hansen. It has always seemed to me to possess a measure of appeal. Throughout this book, I have been at pains to argue that with rising wealth and industrialized living, the need for public services advances, and probably faster than living standards. In part this reflects simply the familiar fact that the demand for services tends to expand faster than the demand for goods. In part, the social conditions of modern life are also accountable for the growing need for government services. Private business is learning to meet many of these new needs—for instance in the field of insurance. It is not inconceivable that some day we shall become rich enough to be able to indulge increasingly a preference for privately supplied services. But at present, and as far ahead as one can see, the trend seems the other way. I would footnote this reference by observing that to recognize a rising trend in the need for public services and to claim that at present we have too little of them, are two different things. The more than doubling of federal and also of state and local expenditures since 1950 should drive home that distinction.

The thesis that public services are neglected and private consumption inflated with trivia has found its most eloquent interpretation in *The Affluent Society* by John Kenneth Galbraith, to whom we were previously indebted for important insights into the workings of American capitalism. Galbraith argues that this imbalance is nourished by advertising, which creates artificial wants. He sees it further accentuated by an obsession with production, which keeps us from realizing that our problems are not those of want, but of affluence. The imbalance is epitomized by our supposed tendency to limit public expenditures to what is strictly essential, while we apply no such criterion to private expenditures.

TOO MANY TRIVIA?

One may reasonably argue that Galbraith exaggerates the distorting influence of advertising. That would not alter the basic assumption on which his thesis rests—the assumption that there are better wants and worse wants. Scientific detachment notwithstanding, I find it extraordinarily difficult to disagree with this proposition. To rate an attendance at the opera and a visit to an (inexpensive) nightclub as equivalents, because the market puts a similar price on them, goes against my grain. So does the equation of a dollar's worth of education and a dollar's worth of chromium on an automobile. And a plausible case would probably be made, on the basis of the evolution of the species, that opera and education do represent more advanced forms of consumption.

But what consequences, if any, should be drawn from such judgment? It is one thing to be irritated by certain manifestations of our contemporary civilization—the gadgets, the chrome, the tail fins and the activities that go with them. It is quite another—and something of a *non sequitur*—to conclude from this that the only alternative to foolish private spending is public spending. Better private spending is just as much of a possibility.

And does this judgment yield a basis for trying to discourage the growth of the less "good" expenditures? In a free society, we obviously want to move with the utmost circumspection. It is worth remembering that even Thorstein Veblen, who went to some extreme in deriding the "leisure class" and its "conspicuous consumption," did not take an altogether negative view of all conspicuous waste. In *The Theory of the Leisure Class* he said, "No class of society, not even the most abjectly poor, foregoes all customary conspicuous consumption. . . . There is no class and no country that has yielded so abjectly before the pressure of physical want as to deny themselves all gratification of this higher or spiritual need."

For fair appraisal of the case against trivia, we would also want to know the approximate size of the bill that is being incurred for various frills and frivolities. Gadgets in cars and homes have drawn the special ire of the critics. It is interesting to note, therefore, that expenditures for all kinds of durable consumer goods, including automobiles, run about 14 per cent of personal consumption. The greater part of this, presumably, goes for the essential parts of fairly essential equipment. What is left for ornaments and gadgets does not loom impressively large. After all, not all the income in this country is spent by people for whom life begins at $25,000. The median family income is $5,600. Would the critics of the affluent society want to live on much less than that?

Whatever our private feelings about the gadgetry in our life, we probably do well not to stress them too hard. It is only too easy for some members of a community to work themselves into a fit of righteousness and to feel tempted to help the rest regulate their existence. In an extreme form, and not very long ago, this happened in the United States with the introduction of prohibition. Some of us may lean toward special taxation of luxuries, but surely no one wants sumptuary legislation banishing from our show windows and homes the offending contrivances. A new puritanism directed against wasteful consumption, however understandable, would make no great contribution to an economy that requires incentive goods to activate competition and free markets. Neither would it be compatible with the freedom that we value.

ENDS AND MEANS

It is the positive side of the case—the asserted need for more public services—that must chiefly concern us. My contention here will be that to talk in terms of "public vs. private" is to confuse the issue. More than that, it is to confuse means and ends. The choice between public and private money is primarily a choice of means. The sensible approach for those who are dissatisfied with some of the ends to which private money is being spent, is to specify first what other ends are important and why. Having determined the ends, the next step is to look to the means. That is the order in which I propose to proceed here.

The critics are right in pointing out that new material needs have been carried to the fore by social and economic evolution— even though they mislabel them as public needs. In the good old days, when this was still a nation of farmers, most people had no serious retirement worries, there was no industrial unemployment problem, good jobs could be had without a college degree, most diseases were still incurable—in short, social security, education, and health care found primitive and natural solutions within the family and among the resources of the neighborhood. Today, these solutions are neither adequate nor usually even possible.

Mounting wealth and advancing technology have brought within reach the means of meeting these needs. We can afford to live better in every way—more creature comforts, more leisure, more attention to matters of the mind and spirit. At the same time we can take better care of retirement, of unemployment, of illness, of education, of the possibilities opened by research, than ever before.

There are indeed new needs. The citizen-taxpayer has his choice of meeting them, as well as all his other needs, in one of two ways. He can buy the goods or services he wants privately, for cash or credit. Or he can buy them from the government, for taxes.

The nation as a whole pays taxes to buy public services as it pays grocery bills to buy groceries. The tax burden may be heavier for some individuals than for others. But the nation as a whole has no more reason to complain about the "burden" of taxes than about the "burden" of grocery bills—and no more reason to hope for relief.

Of the two stores, the private store today still is much the bigger. The public store is smaller, but it is growing faster.

Each store has some exclusive items. The private store sells most of the necessities and all of the luxuries of life, and in most of these has no competition from the government side. The public store has some specialties of its own: defense, public order and justice, and numerous local services that the private organization has not found profitable. But there is a wide range of items featured by both stores: provision for old age, health services, education, housing, development of natural resources.

THE NEW NEEDS

The bulk of the new needs are in this competitive area. The fashionable notion is to claim them all for the public store and to label them public needs. The statistics say otherwise. They say in fact two things: First, the supply of this group of goods and services has expanded very rapidly in recent years; and second, they are being offered, in varying degrees, both by the private and the public suppliers. Let us run down the list.

Provision for old age is predominantly private. The average American family, realizing that while old age may be a burden, it is the only known way to achieve a long life, takes care of the matter in three ways: (1) by private individual savings—home ownership, savings deposits, securities; (2) by private collective savings—life insurance, corporate pension funds; and (3) by public collective savings through social security. Statisticians report that the two collective forms are advancing faster than the individual. The increases far exceed the rise in the Gross National Product of almost 80 per cent (in current prices) over the past ten years; they do not indicate either that these needs are neglected or that they are necessarily public in character.

Education: the bulk of it is public; but a good part, particularly of higher education, is private. Total expenditures for all education have advanced in the last ten years from $9.3 billion to $24.6 billion ($19.3 billion of it public). Education's share in the national income has advanced from 3.8 per cent to 5.8 per cent. The silly story that we spend more on advertising than on education is a canard, though with its gross of over $10 billion, advertising does take a lot of money.

Health expenditures are still mainly private. At considerable expense, it is now possible to live longer and be sick less frequently or at least less dangerously. In the past, most people paid their own doctors' bills, although health care for the indigent has always been provided by public action or private philanthropy. Since the war, the proliferation of health insurance has given some form of collective but private insurance to three-quarters of our 182 million people. This has greatly reduced pressure for a national health service along British lines. For the aging, whose health-care needs stand in inverse proportion to their capacity to pay or insure, public insurance has finally been initiated and needs to be expanded. The total annual expenditure on health is estimated at over $25 billion, a little more than on education. Of this, about $6 billion is public.

So much for the allegation that the "new needs" are all public needs. Now for some further statistics on the public store, which is said to have been neglected. Some of them could make an investor in private growth stocks envious. Research expenditures (mainly for defense and atomic energy) have gone from about $1 billion to over $8 billion in the last ten years. Federal grants to the states have advanced from $2.2 billion to $7 billion during the same period. Social-security benefits rose from $1 billion to over $10 billion. All in all, public cash outlays (federal and state) advanced from $61 billion to $134 billion over ten years, 57 per cent faster than the GNP.

For those who feel about public spending the way Mark Twain felt about whiskey, these figures may still look slim. (Mark Twain thought that while too much of anything was bad, too much whiskey was barely enough.) To others, the data may suggest that the advocates of more public spending have already had their way. Could their present discontent be the result of not keeping their statistics up-to-date? In one of his recent pamphlets, Arthur M. Schlesinger, Jr., claims that the sum of the many neglects he observes (including defense) could be mended by raising public expenditures by $10 to $12 billion. That is well below the increase in public cash outlays that actually did take place in one single fiscal year, from $118.2 billion in 1958 to $132.7 billion in 1959. In the three fiscal years 1957–59, these outlays went up more than $31 billion, though the advance slowed down in 1960. More facts and less indignation might help to attain better perspective.

Some parts of federal, state, and local budgets have expanded less rapidly than those cited—in many cases fortunately. The massive buildup in defense expenditures from the late 'forties to the 'fifties has squeezed other programs. Unfortunately, on the other hand, some programs that both political parties have favored—including aid to education, to depressed areas, for urban renewal—have been delayed unduly by the vicissitudes of politics. But the figures as a whole lend little support to the thesis that politicians don't spend enough, and that the government store is not expanding fast enough.

THE CITIZEN IN THE STORES

The two stores—private and public—work very hard these days to capture the business of the citizen-taxpayer. Here is what he hears as he walks into the private store:

"The principal advantage of this store," the private businessman says, "is that you can shop around and buy exactly what you want. If I don't have it I'll order it. You, the consumer, are the boss here. To be sure, I'm not in business for charity but for profit. But my profit comes from giving you what you want. And with competition as fierce as it is, you can be sure the profit won't be excessive."

If the proprietor has been to Harvard Business School, he will perhaps remember to add something about the invisible hand which in a free economy causes the self-seeking of competitors to work for the common good. He will also, even without benefit of business school, remember to drop a word about the danger of letting the public store across the street get too big. It might endanger freedom.

As the citizen turns this sales talk over in his mind, several points occur to him. Without denying the broad validity of the argument, he will note that quite often he has been induced to buy things he did not really need, and possibly to neglect other, more serious needs. Snob appeal and built-in obsolescence promoted by expensive advertising don't seem to him to fit in with the notion that the consumer is king. Looking at the brand names and patents and trademarks, he wonders whether most products are produced and priced competitively instead of under monopoly conditions. The invisible hand at times seems to be invisible mainly because it is so deep in his pocket.

Bothered by these doubts, the citizen walks across the street and enters the public store.

"Let me explain to you," says the politician who runs it—with the aid of a horde of hard-working bureaucrats doing the chores. "The principles on which this store is run are known as the political process, and if you happen to be familiar with private merchandising they may seem unusual, but I assure you they work. First of all, almost everything in this store is free. We simply assess our customers a lump sum in the form of taxes. These, however, are based largely on each customer's ability to pay, rather than on what he gets from the store. We have a show of hands from the customers once a year, and the majority decides what merchandise the store is to have in stock. The majority, incidentally, also decides how much everybody, including particularly the minority, is to be assessed for taxes.

"You will observe," the politician continues, "that this store is not run for profit. It is like a co-operative, run for the welfare of the members. I myself, to be sure, am not in politics for charity, but for re-election. But that means that I must be interested in your needs, or you would not vote for me. Moreover, there are some useful things that only I can do, with the help of the political process, and in which you and every citizen have an interest. For instance, everybody ought to go to school. I can make them go. Everybody ought to have old-age insurance. I can make that compulsory too. And because I don't charge the full cost of the service, I can help even up a little the inequalities of life.

"By the way," the politician concludes, "if there is any special little thing you want, I may be able to get it for you, and of course it won't cost you a nickel."

The citizen has some fault to find with the political process too. He notes that there is not even a theoretical claim to the benefits of an invisible hand. Majority rule may produce benefits for the majority, but how about the other 49 per cent? Nor is there the discipline of competition, or the need for profits, to test economy of operation. There is no way, in the public store, of adjusting individual costs and benefits. And the promise to get him some small favor, while tempting, worries him, because he wonders what the politician may have promised to others. The political process, he is led to suspect, may be a little haphazard.

He asks himself how political decisions get to be made. Sometimes, obviously, it is not the majority that really makes a decision, but a small pressure group that is getting away with something. He will remember that—after payments for major national security and public debt interest—the largest single expenditure in the federal budget is for agriculture, and the next for veterans. He may also recall that one of the first budgetary actions of the new Administration was to increase funds for agriculture by $3 billion.

THE EXPANDING BELT

Next, the citizen might consider the paralyzing "balance-of-forces" effect that often blocks a desirable reshuffling of expenditures. The allocation of public funds reflects the bargaining power of their sponsors, inside or outside the government. A classical example was the division of funds that prevailed in the Defense Department during the late 'forties. Army, Navy, and Air Force were to share in total resources in a way that would maximize military potential. By some strange coincidence, maximum potential was always achieved by giving each service the same amount of money. It took the Korean War to break this stalemate.

What is the consequence of the balance-of-forces effect? If the proponents of one kind of expenditure want to get more money for their projects, they must concede an increase also to the advocates of others. More education means more highways, instead of less; more air power means more ground forces. To increase a budget in one direction only is as difficult as letting out one's belt only on one side. The expansion tends to go all around. What this comes down to is that politicians are not very good at setting priorities. Increases in good expenditures are burdened with a political surcharge of less good ones.

The last-ditch survival power of federal programs is a specially illuminating instance of the balance of forces. If a monument were built in Washington in memory of each major federal program that has been discontinued, the appearance of the city would not be greatly altered. In contrast, when the Edsel doesn't sell, production stops. But the government is still reclaiming land to raise more farm surpluses and training fishermen to enter an occupation that needs subsidies to keep alive. Old federal programs never die, they don't even fade away—they just go on.

The citizen will remember also the ancient and honorable practice of logrolling. The unhappy fate of the Area Development bill illustrates it admirably. As originally proposed, the bill sought to aid a limited number of industrial areas where new jobs were badly needed. It got nowhere in the Congress. Only when it was extended to a large number of areas with less urgent or quite different problems, were enough legislators brought aboard to pass it. Because of the heavy political surcharge with which it had become loaded, President Eisenhower vetoed the bill. A bill was finally enacted early this year, long after aid should have been brought to the areas that needed it.

Finally, the citizen might discover in some dark corner of his mind a nagging thought: Any particular government program may be a blessing, but could their cumulative effect be a threat to freedom? He has heard businessmen say this so often that he has almost ceased to pay attention to it. He rather resents businessmen acting the dog in the manger, trying to stop useful things from being done unless they can do them. He is irritated when he hears a man talk about freedom who obviously is thinking about profit. And yet—is there any conclusive rebuttal?

THE CITIZEN'S FAILURES

The citizen would be quite wrong, however, if he blamed the politician for the defects of the political process. The fault lies with the process, or better with the way in which the process, the politician, and the citizen interact. The citizen therefore would do well to examine some of his own reactions and attitudes.

First, when he thinks about taxes, he tends to think of them as a burden instead of as a price he pays for a service. As a body, the nation's taxpayers are like a group of neighbors who decide to establish a fire department. Because none is quite sure how much good it will do him, and because each hopes to benefit from the contribution of the rest, all are prudent in their contributions. In the end they are likely to wind up with a bucket brigade.

But when it comes to accepting benefits, the citizen-taxpayers act like a group of men who sit down at a restaurant table knowing that they will split the check evenly. In this situation everybody orders generously; it adds little to one's own share of the bill, and for the extravagance of his friends he will have to pay anyhow. What happens at the restaurant table explains—though it does not excuse—what happens at the public trough.

Finally, in his reaction to public or free services, the citizen takes a great deal for granted, and seldom thinks of the cost. Public beaches mistreated, unmetered parking space permanently occupied, veterans' adjustment benefits continued without need —as well as abuses of unemployment compensation and public assistance—are some examples. This applies also, of course, to privately offered benefits, under health insurance, for instance. The kindly nurse in the hospital—"Why don't you stay another day, dearie, it won't cost you anything, it's all paid for by Blue Cross"—makes the point.

By removing the link between costs and benefits, the political process also reduces the citizen's interest in earning money. The citizen works to live. If some of his living comes to him without working, he would be less than rational if he did not respond with a demand for shorter hours. If these public benefits increase his tax burden so that his over-all standard of living remains unchanged, the higher taxes will reduce his work incentive. Why work hard, if much of it is for the government?

THE POLITICAL DOLLAR AT A DISCOUNT

These various defects of the political process add up to an obvious conclusion: the dollar spent by even the most honest and scrupulous of politicians is not always a full-bodied dollar. It often is subject to a discount. It buys less than it should because of the attrition it suffers as it goes through the process, and so may be worth only 90 cents or 80 cents and sometimes perhaps less. The private dollar, in too many cases, may also be worth less than 100 per cent. But here each man can form his own judgment, can pick and choose or refuse altogether. In the political process, all he can do is say Yes or No once a year in November.

The discount on the public dollar may be compensated by the other advantages of government—its ability to compel, to subsidize, to do things on a big scale and at a low interest cost. Whether that is the case needs to be studied in each instance. Where these advantages do not apply, the private market will give better service than the political process. For many services, there is at least some leeway for choice between the private and public store—health and retirement, housing, research, higher education, natural-resource development. Defense, on the other hand, as well as public administration, public works of all kinds, and the great bulk of education—while perhaps made rather expensive by the political process—leave no realistic alternative to public action.

The argument I have offered is no plea to spend more or less on any particular function. It is a plea for doing whatever we do in the most effective way.

The Effects of Taxation on Work Incentives

GEORGE F. BREAK

George F. Break is Professor of Economics at the University of California, Berkeley. He was one of the panelists appearing before a Congressional subcommittee who contributed papers to the compendium Federal Tax Policy for Economic Growth and Stability.

THE POINT of view that high income-tax rates such as have prevailed in this country since World War II seriously sap the work incentives of the American people and thereby deter economic growth has been presented with great vigor and persistence. Typically the conclusion is treated as self-evident or as so reasonable, given a little thought, as to eliminate the need for direct empirical evidence. One may admire the strategy of this line of attack, but further investigation shows the forces involved in it to be largely illusory.

The first three sections of this paper are concerned with the economic factors which determine the influence on work incentives of the taxation of earned income. It will be seen that there are at least as good reasons for believing that such taxation will have a net incentive effect as there are for believing it will have a disincentive effect. In the next two sections a similar analysis is applied to income taxes on property incomes and to excise and sales taxes. Finally, the findings of a number of recent empirical studies of worker behavior are examined briefly. The results are likely to surprise those who have accepted the disincentive argument as conclusive. High income taxes, it would appear, have as yet not had any serious disincentive effects. It is true that some workers have been led to contract their efforts, but at the same time others have been induced to work both harder and longer. Whatever the merits of fiscal policies aimed at lowering income-tax rates may be, the encouragement of greater productive activity on the part of workers does not appear to be one of them.

INCENTIVE AND DISINCENTIVE EFFECTS OF
INCOME TAXATION

To many taxpayers the disincentive proposition given at the beginning of this paper probably appears realistic enough. They
may reason that "with tax rates as high as they are now it is not
worth my while to do any extra work because the income from
it after taxes is inadequate." The implication, of course, is that
at lower tax rates the additional work would be undertaken. In
reaching this conclusion, however, the taxpayer is likely to be
thinking in terms of a given base income to which a larger reward
from a given amount of extra work is added when tax rates are
lowered. This argument overlooks an important fact—that lower
tax rates would increase the taxpayer's base income—and at
higher income levels, as empirical studies have shown, people
typically want to take more leisure time rather than less. A lowering of income-tax rates, in short, exerts two opposing influences
on work incentives: a stimulating one because after-tax rates
of pay are higher, and a discouraging one because for a given
amount of work taxpayers have more money. Conversely, an increase in tax rates, by lowering wage rates, tends on the one hand
to induce greater effort because taxpayers find themselves with
less money to spend, but, on the other, makes added effort less
attractive by reducing the reward.

Some workers may react to higher taxes by simply tightening
their belts, preferring to economize on consumer goods and services and on saving rather than on leisure time. Others may work
more, thereby economizing on leisure as well as on other things.
Still others may work less, illustrating the disincentive effects of
tax increases. These people, it may be noted, show a marked lack
of attachment to the rewards from productive activity, since they
are led by a fall in earned income as a result of taxation to cut
their incomes still further by reducing their efforts. Such a reaction is, of course, possible. To elevate possibilities of this sort to
the rank of inevitabilities, as some of the more ardent critics of
income taxation are prone to do, seems, however, more than a
little extreme.

Another way of describing the effects of income taxes on work
incentives is in terms of the value to the worker of the disposable

income obtainable from the last unit of work he does. "Value" in this case does not refer simply to the number of dollars earned but more fundamentally to the usefulness of those dollars to the worker and his family. When tax rates rise the value received from a unit of effort is reduced since fewer dollars are brought home to the family coffers, but the usefulness of each dollar is increased since the family has fewer total dollars to spend. If, on balance, the value of the income earned by the last unit of effort decreases, the worker will tend to work less as a result of the increased tax rates; if, on the other hand, the value increases he will continue to work as much as before and may well wish to expand his supply of labor. Opposite results occur when tax rates are lowered. Again we note the existence of opposing lines of influence and the indeterminacy of the final outcome at this level of analysis.

High income taxes, then, do not necessarily have important disincentive effects. Some workers, it is true, may work less hard because of the influence of high tax rates. Others, however, may be led to increase their efforts, and a good many people may be virtually unaffected. Additional evidence is needed before any useful conclusions can be drawn. Fortunately, both theory and observation can help provide that evidence.

THE EFFECTS OF INFLEXIBLE MONETARY COMMITMENTS

Most of us have more than a nodding acquaintance with relatively fixed monetary commitments of one kind or another. Monthly payments on a home mortgage or rental to a landlord, life-insurance premiums, contributions to pension and annuity funds or to prepaid medical plans, union or professional dues, and other fixed costs of earning income, periodic payments incurred when consumer durables are bought on time, the obligation to support and educate children or to care for elderly relatives—all fall in this category. Possession of such commitments tends to make the taxpayer react to an increase in income taxes by increasing his efforts to earn income. The disincentive effect of lower take-home rates of pay is more than offset by the incentive push of a lower level of income when living expenses are not easily contracted.

High income taxes, therefore, are likely to have incentive effects on workers with large families, on young people who are setting up homes and acquiring their stock of consumer durables, and upon all who, for whatever reason, have become heavily indebted to others. A period following a rapid rise in consumer and mortgage debt, when higher taxes may well be called for because of strengthening inflationary pressures, is relatively favorable to the imposition of higher income taxes since their incentive effects will be intensified and their disincentive effects lessened by the previous growth in fixed-debt obligations. For similar reasons, a high and rising birthrate is favorable to high income taxes. On the other hand, Government policies which reduce the pressure of fixed monetary commitment on the worker, such as baby bonuses, provision for old age and retirement, for temporary periods of unemployment, or for sickness and injury tend, by themselves, to strengthen the disincentive effects of income taxation. These adverse tendencies, however, will be offset to the extent that Government benefits of this sort are closely matched by contributions on the part of the beneficiary.

A worker is also effectively committed to the maintenance of a given level of living in the face of an increase in income taxes if that level of living represents the minimum necessary for continued physical existence in his society. On the lowest income groups, therefore, income taxes may be expected to have incentive effects. At higher income levels the purely physical pressure of minimum subsistence is absent, but it may be replaced by equally effective social pressures—well-defined modes and standards of living which the workers feel they must maintain.

Fixed monetary commitments of various kinds, therefore, exist at all income levels. Together they provide an important set of factors which strengthen the incentive effects of high income taxes at the expense of the disincentive effects.

THE EFFECTS OF CHANGES IN PERSONAL EXEMPTION
ALLOWANCES

A raising or lowering of personal exemption allowances has a powerful effect upon income-tax revenues because of the large proportion of income taxed at the lowest bracket rates. Such changes are also likely to affect work incentives. Unfortunately we can specify the result definitely only for those who remain in the same tax bracket both before and after personal exemptions are altered. For them the marginal rate of tax, and hence take-home rates of pay on the last units of work done as well as on any additional units that might be done, remains constant, while disposable incomes rise or fall as exemption allowances rise or fall. The sole effect on incentives, therefore, comes from the changes in disposable income, larger exemptions tending to reduce effort and smaller exemptions to increase it.

A large number of taxpayers, however, will be shifted into a different tax bracket when personal exemptions are changed. For them both marginal and average tax rates—i. e., take-home rates of pay and disposable incomes—change, and opposing influences on work incentives are again set in motion. Increased exemptions, for example, stimulate desires for more leisure time as a result of increased disposable incomes, but increased rates of pay at the margin make work more attractive. The strength of the latter effect will differ at different points on the income scale since rate changes from one tax bracket to the next are not uniform. By far the largest change, of course, occurs at the bottom of the tax scale where the rate plummets from 20 percent to zero for the income receiver who moves down out of the first bracket.

The net incentive or disincentive effect of a given change in personal exemptions, therefore, will depend upon the extent to which taxpayers are concentrated at the boundaries of the various tax brackets rather than at the centers. For those at the boundaries the effect may go either way, but those at the centers will be induced to work harder by reduced exemption allowances and to work less by greater exemptions. A relatively even distribution of taxpayers over the various tax brackets, therefore, would create the presumption that lower exemptions are favorable to work incentives and higher exemptions unfavorable. On the other hand, a significant concentration at the bracket boundaries, especially at the bottom of the lowest bracket, could easily produce exactly the opposite result.

THE TAX TREATMENT OF PROPERTY INCOMES

Another relevant issue to be taken into consideration in studying the incentive effects of any income tax is the treatment of incomes which are more or less independent of any labor services rendered by the income receiver. At given levels of yield—and this is the only important comparison to make—a general income tax which treats all types of income equally will be more favorable to work incentives than one which exempts some property incomes entirely and taxes others only partially.

As compared to the selective tax, the general one taxes certain kinds of property income more heavily but all other types of income less heavily. Since the two taxes are equally productive, taxpayers as a group have the same total disposable income in each case, but under the general tax they realize higher rates of take-home pay from the rendering of labor services. This acts as an incentive to still greater effort. The fact that this kind of tax treats some kinds of property income more severely has little or no effect on work incentives since little or no labor is involved in the creation of these incomes. On the average, therefore, the general tax is more favorable to productive activity. It has the further virtue, of course, of being more equitable since it treats all types of income the same way.

For these reasons policymakers should scrutinize closely proposals which would have the effect of narrowing the base of the individual income tax. If the incomes involved are largely of the property type, the influence of the income tax at given yields is shifted in the disincentive direction. Present provisions concerning capital gains and losses, tax-exempt bond interest, percentage depletion, certain allowable deductions (such as those for meals and the like, which to a large extent are personal consumption on the part of the taxpayer rather than costs of earning income) all tend to make the individual income tax less favorable to work incentives than it would otherwise be.

THE INCENTIVE ASPECTS OF EXCISE AND SALES TAXES

One of the traditional tenets with reference to the relative merits of different kinds of taxes is that excise and sales taxes are more favorable to work incentives than are income taxes. Let us examine this assumption for a moment.

Consider first the probable effects on work incentives of the price changes induced by sales and excise taxes. A general increase in consumer good prices, for example, makes consumers with relatively fixed money incomes worse off and thereby tends to induce more effort.

The rewards from that effort, however, have undergone a reduction in their buying power and so the effort itself is less attractive than it once was. When considering the extra work the worker finds himself both pushed toward it (by his lower real income) and repelled (by the lower real rates of pay) at the same time, and he may in the final analysis expand his labor supply, contract it, or leave it unchanged.

It is true that many consumers may fail to perceive the price changes induced by changes in excise taxes, but they are likely to be much more aware of what it costs them to maintain their accustomed standard of living and what happens to the level of their cash balances in the process. Some evidence of the effects of high prices on worker behavior is provided by a recent British investigation which found that approximately 40 percent of the workers interviewed regarded high prices as a factor which deterred their productive efforts and some 70 percent thought they were also a factor making for greater incentive.[1]

Taxpayers may, of course, do more work not in order to buy additional things but primarily to raise their level of saving. Even in this case, however, the tax-induced price increases are by no means irrelevant. The saving may be specifically earmarked for a future purchase of a taxed good or service. Unless the tax is believed to be temporary, the incentive effect is likely to be the same here as in the case of a person who works in order to consume. Even the person who saves in order to accumulate a certain amount of capital may adjust his goals upward when prices rise.

Finally, excise and sales taxation will affect work incentives in still another way. Such taxes reduce the money incomes of certain income receivers below the levels which would otherwise prevail. An excise tax on watches and clocks, for example, will lower the earning power of workers who are highly skilled in watchmaking, and these effects are likely to spread to all who do the same type of high-precision, fine-scale work. As we have already seen the incentive effects on these people may go either way. Lower income levels induce more effort, but reduced rates of pay have the reverse effect. Until we know more about the types of workers whose incomes are reduced by different kinds of sales and excise taxes and the extent to which these reductions take place, we cannot formulate a complete picture of the incentive-disincentive effects of sales and excise taxation.

1. Royal Commission on the Taxation of Profits and Income, *Second Report*, CMD 9105 (London, 1954), sec. 87.

THE EFFECTS OF LABOR MARKET RIGIDITIES

So far we have not concerned ourselves with the extent to which the worker is free to satisfy his own preferences with regard to the amount of labor services he supplies to the market. The great majority of workers, of course, must either have a full-time job or none at all. We cannot, however, count on this fact to neutralize, for such workers, the potential incentive or disincentive effects of income taxation. For one thing, their preferences may be only temporarily frustrated. Future bargaining with employers may restore the balance. In addition, workers typically have ways of changing their labor supply other than by altering the number of hours worked a week or the number of weeks worked a year. Overtime opportunities may be available and be refused or exploited more fully, other members of the family may enter or leave the labor force, proposed ages of retirement may be altered, or absenteeism on a day-to-day basis may change. These possibilities must be kept in mind in evaluating the results of empirical studies. Inflexible behavior in one area or disincentive effects in another do not necessarily imply either insensitivity or reduced incentives as far as the labor supply as a whole is concerned.

EMPIRICAL STUDIES OF WORK INCENTIVES

Since the pioneering work of Senator Paul H. Douglas [2] in this area, a number of empirical studies of the reactions of workers to changes in their rates of pay have been made. The results, to be sure, are incomplete. We still lack detailed information about the behavior of a number of important worker groups, especially independently employed professional and business people at the middle- to high-income levels, who are both strongly affected by income taxes and able to vary their labor supply more freely than wage earners or salaried personnel. Wage and salary workers, as noted in the preceding section, may vary their supply of labor in a number of different ways, and full information on these various possibilities is not always available even for groups that have been studied rather extensively. In addition, it has frequently been difficult to be certain that the behavior actually observed was due

2. Paul H. Douglas, *The Theory of Wages* (New York, 1934).

to changing pay rates rather than to other factors which also exert an influence on work incentives. Nevertheless, the evidence so far compiled warrants careful consideration because it is both extensive and consistent as to the direction in which it points.[3] For the most part it appears that income taxes exert relatively little influence on work incentives, and that when they do they induce greater effort as frequently as they deter it.

Thomas H. Sanders, for example, concluded, on the basis of an extensive postwar study of executive behavior, that—

the cases in which the evidence showed executives to be working harder were at least equal in number to those indicating less effort, and the former were more definitely recognizable as a tax influence.[4]

In addition, there was evidence that high taxes induced more wives of business executives to enter the labor force and, in general, led the executives themselves to postpone their dates of retirement from active participation in the business. Offsetting these tax incentives, however, was a tendency for some to refuse promotions and advantageous offers from other companies when the change meant greatly increased burdens and relatively little increase in net compensation. Finally, it was noted that a good deal of executive effort was being diverted into a study of tax laws and of ways of reducing tax burdens.

Another study of a small sample of 7 surgeons with incomes between $36,000 and $115,000 led the author to conclude "* * * we would judge that increased taxes have not reduced the surgeons' incentive." [5] He also noted that 4 of the 7 doctors planned, at the time of interview, to retire later than they had previously planned (before World War II) because they had been unable to accumulate sufficient capital. These reactions might be attributed to the influence of higher taxes or higher prices, or both.

It is interesting to note that in a recent British study, although over two-thirds of the male workers interviewed believed that

3. A more detailed summary of the results of studies of the United States labor market up to 1953 is included in the author's "Income Taxes, Wage Rates, and the Incentive To Supply Labor Services," *National Tax Journal,* VI (December 1953), 350–1. More recent investigations are noted in the text below.

4. Thomas H. Sanders, *Effects of Taxation on Executives* (Boston, 1951), p. 20.

5. Robert Davidson, "Income Taxes and Incentive: The Doctor's Viewpoint," *National Tax Journal,* VI (September 1953), p. 297.

as a general matter income taxes discouraged productive effort, less than one-third of them felt that taxes had affected their own personal effort adversely, and almost as many thought the effect was to induce them to work harder.[6] When workers who had turned down an opportunity to work overtime were asked why they had done so, only 5 percent or less of them cited high taxes in reply.[7] The National Coal Board, as a result of a number of studies of absenteeism in the British coal mines, concluded that "Tax considerations were * * * responsible for only one-third of 1 percent of the shifts lost."[8] The Royal Commission itself reached the general conclusion that "the levels of taxation within present limits do not inhibit or induce any significant proportion of the working population to modify their attitudes to their working behavior."[9]

These findings are the more significant since the pressure of taxation is in general greater in Britain than in the United States, the income tax starts at lower levels of income and its rate structure rises more steeply, and British workers are provided with comprehensive low cost medical and dental services which, alone, might be expected to push the influence of income taxes in the disincentive direction. In addition, a recent study shows that central government tax and expenditure programs have carried the redistribution of income further in Britain than in the United States.[10]

CONCLUSIONS

Human motivation is a complex phenomenon no matter what the area of study. People who are keenly interested in their jobs are not likely to be much deterred by even significant changes in

6. Royal Commission on the Taxation of Profits and Income, op. cit., secs. 74 and 81.

A similar result for the United States appears when we contrast Kimmel's 95 percent affirmative response to the question: "Do you believe that the higher the tax rate the less the incentive to work and save?" with the results of Sanders' study of executive behavior. Cf. Lewis H. Kimmel, *Taxes and Economic Incentives* (Washington, 1950), pp. 101–102.

7. Royal Commission on the Taxation of Profits and Income, op. cit., secs. 74 and 81.

8. Ibid, sec. 39.

9. Ibid, p. 115.

10. Allan M. Cartter, *The Redistribution of Income in Postwar Britain— A Study of the Effects of the Central Government Fiscal Program in 1948–49* (New Haven, 1955), especially pp. 91–92.

taxes. Strong personal ambitions may also push even very high income taxes into the background. Workers in a society that is alert and active and progressing rapidly may not be deterred in their efforts by taxation, whereas workers in a stagnant and disillusioned society might well be. Strong public support for what the Government is doing and a widespread belief that it is accomplishing its objectives in an efficient and honest manner may tend to impart favorable incentive aspects to taxation. Cultural and religious patterns, by imposing on the individual certain habits of thought and action, may govern his reactions to taxation of various kinds, and so on.

In spite of the complexities, we are by no means completely at sea. Careful empirical studies have been made and, incomplete as the results still are, it is encouraging to note that neither in Great Britain nor in the United States is there any convincing evidence that current high levels of taxation are seriously interfering with work incentives. There are, in fact, as indicated above, a number of good reasons for believing that considerably higher taxes could be sustained without injury to worker motivation should the need arise. Conversely, the social and economic need for strong work incentives does not, at the moment, make imperative a reduction in Government expenditures or an expansion in the role of excise and sales taxation in order to bring about a reduction in income taxes.

On State Expenditure

BERTRAND DE JOUVENEL

Bertrand de Jouvenel is a contemporary French political philosopher. His book The Ethics of Redistribution, *in which this essay appears, is a critique of the welfare state.*

THE PRODUCTIVITY OF PRIVATE EXPENDITURE

THE CONCEPTS of income as the means to consumer-satisfaction and as a reward for productive effort are in economics complementary, but they do not exhaust the reality of income. It is only if one pictures society as a kitchen-cum-hall stage set, where the actors can be seen on the one hand broiling some indistinguishable 'stuff' which on the other hand they absorb, that we can be content with these two notions of income. But in fact, to keep to our theatrical comparison, what we took for the stage is only back-stage. True, the actors are busy producing the stuff that they are also consuming, eating, spreading upon their faces, turning into props, whatever you will; but this only in order to strut upon the stage. In other terms, consumption is not the ultimum, the final outcome of production; it also can be regarded as mere means to the real ultimum: human life.

Men's lives are surely to man as student the important phenomenon in society, the thing of beauty or at least of interest. Consumption is merely the means of supporting these lives. To the social philosopher interested in human beings it must seem absurd that one should be passionately interested in equalizing among these lives supplies of the 'stuff', on the ground that absorbing the stuff is the stuff of life. . . .

Gnawing the Income-Bone · The notion of income as means to consumer-satisfaction assumes two things: that consumption is *asocial* and that it is *unproductive*. It must be asocial, be pleasurable or profitable to the income holder alone: under such conditions indeed there is no perceptible reason for allowing Primus more selfish satisfaction than Secundus. And it must be unproductive: why should Primus make a trip to Italy and not Secundus? Why indeed, if both are merely bent on pleasure jaunts? But should Primus be a young architect seeking to familiarize himself with Renaissance designs, surely his tour is not to be set on the same footing as the pleasure jaunt of Secundus!

The notion of income as means to consumer-enjoyment implies that the individual, his day's work done, his debt to society discharged, retires to masticate his income-bone in seclusion, a selfish gastric process, leading nowhere.

But it is not so. Living is a social process. Our individual life is not for ourselves alone. A generous spirit will render many services to society outside his professional activities. A professor's open table may be a means of education superior to his lectures, or complementary to them. Individual income, socially consumed, is a means to such services. These are not accounted as productive services, because they are free. The misleading picture of national income takes into account only services on which a commercial price is put. This is blinding us to the destruction of values which are not commercialized.

Further, the metaphor of the income-bone ignores the salient fact that consumption is to a large extent necessary outlay to bring forth productive activities.

From the scrap-heap of discarded notions let us for a moment rescue the 'iron law of wages', from which Marx derived his celebrated error that all the employer pays for is the cost of reproduction of the labourer's force. The 'iron-law' wage just allows the labourer to keep fit for his task. If we focus our attention on such a wage we may properly state that it includes no net income and that only whatever the worker in fact receives over and above such a wage can be accounted net income. Acting upon this assumption, practically all fiscal systems allow a basic deduction from income, this being exempt from taxation.

Proceeding therefrom, we may be tempted to say that for all income recipients there is the same basic need to be met, above which net income begins: and this is in fact the prevailing system. This idea of identical basic needs has been encouraged by its evident truth in the case of our lower functions, and by the consequent justifiable practice of food rationing.

But the reasoning is in fact very faulty: keeping a man physically fit and keeping him fit for diverse social duties are not identical notions. The same basic expenditure on basic needs which keeps a common labourer fit for his job will prove inadequate to keep a Treasury official fit for his specific task. Each specific task calls for 'functional expenditure', which is in fact cost of production and should not enter into net income.[1] . . . Social history teaches us that what we have of civilization was bought at an enormous cost, the *élites* from which we derive our culture having been supported by sweated masses—a subject on which Bakunin, among others, wrote most eloquent pages. Even in our day we meet the problem when we very properly concern ourselves with Asiatic or African populations. These can only progress through investment in *élites* as well as investment in machines. The present tendency is to provide such investments from foreign funds. But if western riches were unavailable, the choice would be between sweating their equivalent out of the mass of lower incomes or leaving matters as they are.

This point need not be laboured: it is clear enough that progress is linked with the existence of *élites*, the production and upkeep of which are costly, and the incomes of which could not be flattened out without great social loss.

The Treatment of Corporate Bodies Compared to That of Families · The egalitarian trend notwithstanding, it is generally agreed that men fulfilling certain functions need considerable means, and eventual amenities which fit them to render their specific services. But such expenditure is regarded in an entirely different light, depending on whether it is assumed by these men out of their incomes, or assumed for them by *ad hoc* institutions.

Here we come up against the feeling so prevalent in our day, that corporate bodies may do what individuals may not and that partakers in corporate existence may thereby enjoy privileges which would be denied them in their capacity as mere individuals.

Corporate bodies, *personae fictae,* enjoy in our day a quite fantastic preference over real people. The firm produces the goods, the family produces the people. It is puzzling that the needs of the former should be so well understood by the law-makers, and the needs of the latter so disregarded. It seems that law-makers can picture only the firm as an institution with a purpose and therefore respectable. The income recipient, on the other hand, his day's work done, is seen as going round the booths of a fair, blueing his rights to consumer-satisfaction. It

1. It is only the 'surplus' of incomes which one can reasonably think of equalizing.

is not realized that he is an entrepreneur in his own right. He marries, sets up a house, raises children and, it is to be assumed, struggles to bring himself and his family to the greatest possible degree of accomplishment. His achievement is to be recognized as useful to society in that he fits himself and his descendants for their roles as producers: in this respect it is an indirect contribution to the raising of national income. But the matter is not to be taken from that angle only: his achievement is far more than a contribution to *another* end, it is an end *per se*, it is *the* end of a 'good society' or a major part of it.

It is incomprehensible to the point of scandal that public authority should facilitate the upkeep of a tawdry picture or variety theatre, but not the upkeep of a great house, a thing of aesthetic and ethical value, out of which have come generations of the men who have made England what it is. Out of cinema takings, the wherewithal to preserve the cinema in its present state is deducted from taxable income. This is not so in the case of a home, and there is no reason for it other than the legislator's blind spot. It is not to be excused on the grounds that commercial ventures must be favoured over family ventures, the former being of such a nature that no one would embark upon them were they as ill-treated as the latter; for non-profit-making institutions enjoy even better treatment than commercial ventures. The family is such an institution; but as a natural body it is denied the advantages afforded to artificial bodies. . . .

Purposeful Expenditures the State's Privilege · The case for productive consumption is so strong that all opinions coincide on this point. If leftism is unwilling to take account of productive consumption in its treatment of personal incomes, it is not out of indifference to formative expenditure, but because this is regarded as henceforth the State's business. There is no sympathy for the father who spends vast sums on his son's education, and they are not accepted as costs deductable from taxable income, because the father need not, and some would say should not, bear this expenditure. The State will see to it that the boy gets the education, if state auditors so decide. The expense, and the decision, are to be taken out of private hands. It does not matter that personal incomes are so amputated as to become incapable of bearing constructive costs. They need not do so, and more precisely they are not meant to. Let the income recipient spare himself the trouble, thus recuperating net income to squander; the public authority will fulfil such of these individual purposes as are found worthy.

This attitude tends to turn personal incomes into a sum made up of the means of physical support plus pocket money. The citizen thereby loses a fundamental social responsibility: that of contributing in his private capacity to the advancement of his dependents and of his surroundings. He is encouraged to become something like a maintenance man. In so far as he adopts this attitude, equalization of incomes becomes justified. If surplus over mere cost of physical needs is to be spent at the races, why indeed should one have a greater surplus than the other?

While heads of families must perforce cease to provide accomplished and useful members of society, and are shorn of their power to advance society by their individual efforts, the State assumes full responsibility. How does it discharge it, and at what cost?

It does not see to everything, and, for instance, fails to build up homes which are an education in themselves. It does, however, spend a lot of money, and in the process it destroys the incomes of the upper and middle classes without building up those of the working classes.

A High Degree of Taxation in All Ranges · A thoroughgoing and consistent egalitarianism would redistribute incomes equally and let subsequent effects take their course. If, in such circumstances, a number of social accomplishments went undemanded, the conclusion would seem to follow that such accomplishments had no place in the 'society of equals'.

We noticed that redistributionists turn their backs on so simple a course and keep up, or even greatly develop from public funds, services which the 'society of equals' would not buy on a free market at anything like the costs assumed by the State.

The clipping of the upper- and middle-class incomes therefore necessitates an increase in public expenditure and in public taxation. [Yet] nothing like the sums which [seem] at first sight available from higher incomes [are] in fact capable of being redistributed, their contributions to the Treasury and to investment having to be deducted. But now a further most important deduction has to be made, in so far as the State proposes to restore out of public funds such formative expenditures as were previously borne by heads of families. Thus a father is not to be spared sufficient income to cover the cost of sending his son to Paris to study painting, but the State may pay for it. It is out of the question to lessen a family's taxation so that it may keep up a historic mansion, but a curator may well be appointed with a proper remuneration. . . .

The Destruction of Free Services · We have noticed that consumption is assumed in the prevailing doctrines to be both unproductive and asocial. We have discussed at some length the productive character of family consumption and seen that in so far as taxation makes productive expenditures difficult for the head of the family, such productive expenditures tend to be pushed on to corporate bodies or assumed by the State.

Let us now attend to the social character of individual, or family, expenditure. The modern statesman understands that engineers, chemists and other such must be trained and kept in a state of fitness, and [he] is quite eager that the State should assume the cost of such people, quite willing that the corporate bodies for whom they work should charge as costs functional facilities and amenities provided to these valuable citizens.

But the individual's value to society does not lie exclusively in the professional services he renders. It would be a sorry society in which men gave nothing to their contemporaries over and above the services for which they are rewarded and which enter into the computation of national income. That would be no society at all. Often enough one has a frightening vision of such a society, when one sees in some suburban train tired men travelling back from the day's toil to the small house in which they will shut themselves up to eat and sleep until they travel back to the factory or to the office. At those moments one treasures what is left of society: warm hospitality, leisured and far-ranging conversation, friendly advice, voluntary and unrewarded services. Culture and civilization, indeed the very existence of society, depend upon such voluntary, unrewarded activities. They are time- and resource-consuming and costly. There seems to be little awareness among us that they have entered upon a precipitous decline.

This decline goes unnoticed in our age of figures, and indeed the phenomenon is paradoxically shown in statistics as an increase. This occurs in so far as previously unrewarded services come to be salaried and are therefore dignified into 'output'.

Strangely enough, socialists, who dislike valuation by the market, have become dependent for their policies upon an intellectual technique which draws its validity entirely from the valuations of the market. Thereby services freely given have tended to be overlooked as against professional services. The consequences stretch very far: it has often been noted that a man and wife get worse treatment as such than they would as a combination of employer and housekeeper. In the field of public life, disregard of the value of free services works against the very principle of democracy.

Surely it is a most undesirable division of social labour which sets apart a class of public managers as against a mass of passive citizens who then are not truly citizens. Yet what else can happen if mere citizens are left no margin of resources to expend on public activity and at the same time come up against the competition of professionals? It is puzzling that private corporate interests should be allowed to count as legitimate costs propaganda for their special cause, while the citizen is allowed no margin of income with which to further his disinterested championship of the common weal.

The stripping of incomes goes so far that even hospitality tends to be discouraged. As a result of the State's assumption that consumption is *asocial* it tends to become so. The age of socialism turns out to be that in which men are most shut into their individual lives, most confined to their several paths.

Commercialization of Values · An important component of socialism was the ethical revolt against the sordid motivations of a commercial society, where everything, so the saying went, was done for money. It is, then, a paradoxical outcome of socialist policies that the services which were rendered without thought of reward should be on their way to disappearance, a number of these activities being turned into professions and therefore performed for a monetary reward. Only very careless thinking can represent modern society as one in which more and more things are freely given. Services which are paid for in bulk by taxation are not freely given. And how could they be, when the producers of these free services claim salaries equal or superior to those which reward services that the individual buys in the market? The only services which are truly free are those which are rendered by individuals exacting no payment for them: and these are most manifestly on the decline.

An unnoticed consequence of this development is that demand rules far more imperiously in our society of today than it did heretofore. Where there is no margin of leisure and income to enable individuals to offer free services, where all services can be offered only in so far as their performance is paid for, either by individual buyers or by the community, there is no opportunity of proffering services the want of which is not felt by a sufficient number of consumers or by the leaders of the community.

Let us take as an illustration the various investigations into working-class conditions made in the nineteenth century. Such work was at the time susceptible of being rewarded neither by the commercial market nor by the government. It is an arresting thought that the writing of Marx's *Das Kapital* was made possible only by Engels' benefactions out of untaxed profits. Marx did not have to sell his wares on the market, not did he have to get his project accepted by a public foundation of learning. His career testifies to the social utility of surplus incomes. It is of course assumed by *Etatistes* of today that Marx under the new dispensation would benefit from ample and honourable public support. But it seems so to them because his idea is now an old one and is accepted as the prevailing prejudice of our time. An innovator as bold today as he was in his day would not get by the boards of control which administer public funds. . . .

The more one considers the matter, the clearer it becomes that redistribution is in effect far less a redistribution of free income from the richer to the poorer, as we imagined, than a redistribution of power from the individual to the State.

Redistribution an Incentive to Tolerating the Growth of Public Expenditure · Public finance generally is a dull subject, but public finance in the first half of the twentieth century is entrancing: it has been revolutionized and in turn has been the means of a revolution in society. Out of many new aspects of public finance, the two most notable are, first, that it has been used to alter the distribution of the national income between social classes and, second, that the fraction of national income passing through public hands has enormously increased.

The point I propose to make here is that avowed redistributionist policies have made possible the tremendous growth of taxation and public expenditure. The role played by the State in transferring incomes evidently entailed some increase in the volume of public encashing and payments, but this volume has grown out of all proportion to the needs of this function. Such growth has encountered only the weakest opposition; my argument is that a change of mind towards public expenditure has been induced by redistributionist policies, the greatest gainer from which is not the lower-income class as against the higher but the State as against the citizen.

Let us recall that in past phases of history the public authorities have found it difficult not only to increase their fractional share of national income but also, even in a period of rising real or nominal incomes, to retain the same proportion of this income as they previously enjoyed. The revolutions which occurred in Europe between 1640 and 1650, the English Revolution, the Naples revolution, and France's abortive *Fronde,* all seem to be linked with resistance by taxpayers to government demands for more funds in view of the price relvolution. The old attitude of taxpayers was ruled by the desire to keep the government down to its usual takings in nominal terms. It is then almost incredible that, notwithstanding the period of inflation we have gone through, governments of our century should have found it possible to obtain an ever-increasing fraction of the nations' income.

Resistance to taxation has not always been general: the late Stuarts and the late Bourbons kept small groups of pensioners who were all for increasing the load of the many. It was then made one of the cardinal principles of taxation that it was to spare no one and to benefit no special group. These principles were infringed early in this century when the State began to subsidize, albeit modestly, special services for specific groups; simultaneously a new mode of taxation was adopted, surtax, which bore only upon a minority. This was the thin end of a wedge driven into the solidarity of taxpayers. When war demanded a huge increase in the rate of income-tax, this became quite unbearable for the poorer taxpayers, and deductions and allowances were necessary; these were compensated by an increasing steepness of surtax. Thus the very heaviness of taxation made necessary a difference of treatment between the different income classes. When, at the end of the war, the State retained part of its taxation gains, it excused its avidity by providing net ɩdvantages out of taxation to the unfavoured mass. Thus a great increase in state takings and expenditure was made tolerable to the majority by some measure of redistribution, and the process was repeated and enhanced during and after World War II.

It is not meant to imply that any conscious policy of breaking down taxpayer's resistance by advantages given to the poorer majority was at any time pursued by anyone. But the fact is that all the steps in the swelling of the Budget were coupled with increasing inequality of treatment, deductions, allowances and positive benefits for the citizens in the lower-income ranges.

Redistribution Incidental to Centralization? · In our exploration we have found ourselves repeatedly coming across centralization as the major implication of redistributionist policies. In so far as the State amputates higher incomes it must assume their saving and investment functions, and we come to the centralization of investment. In so far as the amputated higher incomes fail to sustain certain social activities, the State must step in, subsidize these activities, and preside over them. In so far as income becomes inadequate for the formation and expenses of those people who fulfil the more intricate or specialized social functions, the State must see to the formation and upkeep of this personnel. Thus the consequence of redistribution is to expand the State's role. And conversely, as we have just seen, the expansion of the State's takings is made acceptable only by measures of redistribution.

We then may well wonder which of these two closely linked phenomena is predominant: whether it is redistribution or centralization. We may ask ourselves whether what we are dealing with is not a political even more than a social phenomenon. This political phenomenon consists in the demolition of the class enjoying 'independent means' and in the massing of means in the hands of managers. This results in a transfer of power from individuals to officials, who tend to constitute a new ruling class as against that which is being destroyed. And there is a faint but quite perceptible trend towards immunity for this new class from some part of the fiscal measures directed at the former.

This leads the observer to wonder how far the demand for equality is directed against inequality itself and is thus a fundamental demand, and how far it is directed against a certain set of 'unequals' and is thus an unconscious move in a change of *élites*.

The "Isms" and Social Technique

ROBERT A. DAHL and CHARLES E. LINDBLOM

Robert A. Dahl and Charles E. Lindblom are Professors of Political Science and Economics respectively at Yale University. Their book Politics, Economics and Welfare, *which is introduced by the following essay, is a study of government policy techniques in a democracy.*

GRAND ALTERNATIVES AND THE "ISMS"

IN ECONOMIC organization and reform, the "great issues" are no longer the great issues, if ever they were. It has become increasingly difficult for thoughtful men to find meaningful alternatives posed in the traditional choices between socialism and capitalism, planning and the free market, regulation and laissez faire, for they find their actual choices neither so simple nor so grand. Not so simple, because economic organization poses knotty problems that can only be solved by painstaking attention to technical details—how else, for example, can inflation be controlled? Nor so grand, because, at least in the Western world, most people neither can nor wish to experiment with the whole pattern of socioeconomic organization to attain goals more easily won. If, for example, taxation will serve the purpose, why "abolish the wage system" to ameliorate income inequality?

Still, the older point of view is not entirely abandoned; it crops up in unexpected places. "The irrational and planless character of society," Erich Fromm writes, "must be replaced by a planned economy. . . ." [1] He does not say, however, what is to be planned, or how, or for what particular purposes; only that "self-realization for the masses of people requires planning."

Even Schumpeter [2] sometimes writes in terms of mythical grand alternatives, introducing, it has appeared to some of his

1. Erich Fromm, *Escape from Freedom*, Rinehart and Co., New York, 1941, p. 272.
2. Joseph A. Schumpeter, *Capitalism, Socialism and Democracy* (2nd ed.), Harper & Brothers, New York, 1947.

readers, "an anthropomorphic supernatural force, capitalism, which becomes the operating force in history." [3] His concept of socialism is in one context sophisticated, in another naïve, because socialism to him is sometimes a product of an accumulation of incremental changes and at other times a system consciously chosen in a particular time and place as an alternative to capitalism. Writing of socialism as planning, he says: "A situation may well emerge in which most people will consider complete planning as the smallest of all possible evils." [4] The starkness of the alternative, the notion of "complete planning" (what can it mean?) are earmarks of a disappearing point of view.

For all their contributions to our understanding of economic organization, Schumpeter, Hayek,[5] Lippmann,[6] Mises,[7] and a host of socialists or planners (to say nothing of the older doctrinaire socialists and communists) are to various degrees enmeshed in the now vanishing tradition of the great "isms." The grand alternatives they envision are the ignes fatui of Right and Left alike. Capitalism is now hardly more than a name stretched to cover a large family of economies in which distant cousins, it is true, resemble one another, but no more than do "capitalist" United States and "socialist" Britain. Socialism once stood for equality; but income and inheritance taxation, social security and other techniques of "capitalist" reform have destroyed its distinction. And in the eyes of socialists themselves, public ownership of industry is now simply an implement in everyone's tool kit for economic reform. Socialism has lost its unique character.

Plan or no plan? Everyone believes in planning in the literal sense of the word; and, for that matter, everyone believes that national governments should execute some plans for economic life. No one favors bad planning. Plan or no plan is no choice at all; the pertinent questions turn on particular techniques: Who shall plan, for what purposes, in what conditions, and by what

3. See Walter Eucken, *The Foundations of Economics*, William Hodge and Company, London, 1950, p. 330.

4. Joseph A. Schumpeter, "The March into Socialism," *American Economic Review*, May, 1950, pp. 446–456.

5. F. A. Hayek, *The Road to Serfdom*, University of Chicago Press, Chicago, 1944.

6. Walter Lippmann, *An Inquiry into the Principles of the Good Society*, Little, Brown and Co., Boston, 1937.

7. Ludwig von Mises, *Human Action*, Yale University Press, New Haven, 1949.

devices? Free market or regulation? Again, this issue is badly posed. Both institutions are indispensable.

Of course great issues remain. Because the whole is sometimes greater than the sum of its parts, another step in a series of reforms may produce more for good or bad than the modest results expected. Reform may pass through breaking points. Even so, further debate on the old alternatives shows no promise of discovering these points, if there are any. Nor does it succeed in turning attention to the countless particular social techniques out of which "systems" are compounded.

VARIETY AND INNOVATION OF SOCIAL TECHNIQUES

In economic life the possibilities for rational social action, for planning, for reform—in short, for solving problems—depend not upon our choice among mythical grand alternatives but largely upon choice among particular social techniques.

The number of alternative politico-economic techniques is tremendously large. For example, the alternative forms of business enterprise are numerous. One is called private enterprise, but its alternative forms in turn are many. Proprietorship, partnership, and corporation are terms suggesting three kinds of alternative structures significantly different one from the others. Corporations may be relatively simple structures for family ownership or complex bureaucracies with or without owner control. And a corporation operating under a minimum of regulation is different from one subject to securities and exchange regulation; different again from one embedded in a matrix of regulations developed through collective bargaining, from one operating under the ever present threat of antitrust action, or from one subject to rate regulation.

Moreover, the number of alternative techniques is constantly growing by discovery, invention, and innovation. Many people think of invention and innovation in technology, but not in social structure; the bias probably accounts for a frequent failure to take account of the increasing possibilities for rational social reform through the improvement of techniques. We need only list a few inventions and discoveries to observe how they have increased the possibilities of rational social action, even if they often bring new problems in their wakes. The corporation itself was once an innovation; so also were unemployment compensation, food stamps, cost accounting, zoning, Lend-Lease, coöperatives, scientific management, points rationing, slum clearance, government old-age pensions, disability benefits, collective bargaining. Their origins are not so far distant that we cannot visualize a kind of accumulation of competence.

The rate of increase in techniques is now extremely rapid. Why this is so must be a matter of speculation until the process of invention of social techniques is systematically studied. One hypothesis is that the growth of democracy has made it possible for masses of people to insist that problems be attacked where earlier the absence of any obvious solution to a problem was sufficient to deter any sustained efforts to solve it.

The process of innovation is both scientific and political. It is not enough that new social techniques be discovered; they must also be put into use. Invention and discovery are only the beginning of a process the next step in which is innovation, a matter of politics. What we are suggesting is that this process taken as a whole is proceeding with astonishing rapidity—it is perhaps the greatest political revolution of our times. Anyone who is not impressed with it can hardly gauge the richness—and dangers— of possible social reform and, failing that, he cannot deal competently with public policy.

Rational and responsible reform may consequently suffer from a serious limitation at the hands of those who fail to grasp the fact that alternatives are many, that new ones can be expected to appear, and that they can be created. One finds in the British debate over broadcasting policy a preoccupation with the British system and American commercial radio as the only two major alternatives; all too seldom attention is given to other alternatives yet to be tried and to still others unknown, yet to be invented. An old saw says that armies are always well prepared to fight the last war. Much of the discussion of social policy suffers from the same disability.

SELECTIVITY IN POLITICO-ECONOMIC TECHNIQUES

The alternative techniques available for a particular problem commonly offer a high degree of selectivity. They permit more precision in choice, more careful adaptation of means to ends, than men sometimes take account of. Consider, for example, the fine gradations in choice of alternative schemes of private enterprise permitted by its multiplicity of forms, existing and conceivable. The refinements in choice permitted by gradations in techniques are not limited to trivial differences among them. They range over a number of continua in which the opposite poles pose such critical alternatives as government power and private power, voluntarism and compulsion, centralization and decentralization, prescription and indoctrination, local determination and national determination.

We can illustrate the array of choices commonly available to policy, each one slightly different from another related to it, and at the same time emphasize once more the large numbers of alternative techniques by diagraming a number of these continua in which the variables are significant and upon which particular techniques suited to some particular problem or goal can be placed. Imagine, for example, the choices open between private ownership and public ownership as polar methods of enterprise organization. Opinions will differ, of course, as to the exact placement of some techniques on such a scale; but despite these differences, the pattern of such a continuum is as in Diagram 1.

The diagram proves nothing; it is only illustrative. Diagram 1 displays something of the variety of techniques possible between an unregulated private enterprise, on the one hand, and a business like the post office run as an ordinary government department, on the other hand. Both to illustrate how "public" ownership and "private" ownership have been stretched in meaning to cover techniques ranging over a long continuum and to show again the invalidity of thinking in terms of comprehensive systems, we have placed the techniques ordinarily associated in the public mind with private enterprise above the line and those commonly associated with socialism below. They overlap; the one set of techniques is not huddled toward one end of the scale, the second set toward the other. Note in particular the placement of "socialized" medicine.

This diagram reveals the foolishness of the debate on nationalization versus private enterprise. It suggests that the Atomic Energy Commission's contractual system may provide more comprehensive public control over enterprises than can be had through the degree of autonomy granted corporations like the nationalized enterprises of Britain or the Port of New York Authority. But whether that is true or not—and we emphasize again that the placement of techniques on such a scale as this must be arbitrary

DIAGRAM 1. A Continuum Showing Some of the Choices Available Between Government Ownership and Private Enterprise

Government ← → **Private**

	C1	C2	C3	C4	C5	C6	C7
Above the line	AEC lease and contract; Some types of defense contracts		Regulated public utilities	Subsidized corporation (regulated like those at right); Anti-trust	Corporation subject to misc. corp. regulation, incl. labor and securities	Corporation subject to corporate regulation	A hypothetical small proprietorship subject only to common law
On the line			Govt. ownership of part of an industry	Joint govt.-private firm			
Below the line	An enterprise operated as an ordinary govt. dept., such as the post office	Public corp. subject to ministerial control — BBC, British RR, TVA, Port of London, Port of N.Y.	Public corp. with tripartite control — French electricity, French RR	Worker control, Guilds, Syndicates	Govt. contracts with private producers, as in public housing	Govt. purchases from private sellers, as in British health program and "socialized" medicine	

Below the line: techniques popularly described with words such as "nationalized," "socialized," "government owned," and "public enterprise."

Above the line: techniques popularly described with words as "private enterprise," "private property," and "free enterprise."

On the line: techniques popularly thought to be neither clearly public nor private.

to a degree—for the particular goals sought, the AEC contractual system, like public utility regulation, worker control schemes, subsidies, or securities and exchange regulation, is often better than the formula of nationalization. But each of these techniques offers a slightly different combination of government and private control, and it is therefore possible to choose that particular combination best suited to remedy a particular organizational deficiency.

Note also that choice can range over even more precise gradations than those shown on the diagram, for many of these alternative techniques offer methods of combining public and private power with respect to any one specific kind of entrepreneurial decision which policy might wish to affect. We have also understated the possibilities of precision in choice because readability requires simplification: in most cases we have placed *types* of enterprise on the scale rather than identifying a particular enterprise. There will actually be found a gradation of choice within the type itself. . . .

Diagram 2 represents choices between voluntary and compulsory organizations for a variety of purposes, an illustration which should make clear that policy is never restricted to the simple choice between calling upon "government" to perform a given function and leaving its performance, on the other hand, to a "private" group. The separation of techniques above and below the line is an incidental reminder that private organizations may be as compulsory as government organizations. The comments on the earlier diagrams should make the meaning of this diagram, as well as of Diagram 3, sufficiently clear without further comment. Diagram 3 is an attempt to show the gradation of choice between procedures closely supervised by central government officials and those possessing a high degree of autonomy. Since government is often widely identified with prescription and private organization with autonomy, a wide range of autonomy-prescription combinations is revealing. The number of these diagrams can be increased indefinitely both by examining other kinds of choices and by examining the same kinds of choices with respect to other problems or goals.

Whether the rapidity of innovation in new techniques of control is or is not the greatest political revolution of our times, techniques and not "isms" are the kernel of rational social action in the Western world. Both socialism and capitalism are dead. The

DIAGRAM 2. *A Continuum Showing Some of the Choices Available Between Voluntary and Compulsory Organizations*

Voluntary ——— **Compulsory**

Advisory councils	Civil service	Contracting members of Agric. Adj. Admin.	NRA code groups	Tax districts	Municipality	An American state	Social security systems	The nation-state
		Guilds and syndicates	Land-use planning districts	Closed-shop union	Class and status groups	Guilds and syndicates		
Small private clubs	Political parties	Professional and business organizations	Union with maintenance-of-membership rule	Business firm where annuity is lost on separation	Business groups with delegated govt. power: e.g., news-print users in Great Britain			
	Pressure groups	Unions						

Above the line: organizations commonly thought of as governmental.
Below the line: organizations commonly thought of as private.

DIAGRAM 3. *A Continuum Showing Some of the Choices Available Among Kinds of Public Agencies According to the Degree to Which the Agency's Operations are Prescribed by a Hierarchical Superior*

Autonomy ← ——————————————————————————————————— → **Prescription**

BBC	Coal Board	Local govt.	Bank of England	Organization and Management Division, Treasury	Courts	Cabinet Secretariat	Stationery Office	Ministry of Pensions
				TVA · Regulatory commissions		Recla-mation Bureau · Budget Bureau · General Acctg. Office		
Autonomous agencies: e.g., trustees of the New Haven commons	Semi-autonomous agencies such as the Port of New York Authority	Atomic Energy Com-mission	Supreme Court	Securities and Exchange Commission	Interstate Commerce Commission		Unem-ployment compen-sation	Veterans' Adminis-tration

Above the line: British governmental agencies.
Below the line: U.S. governmental agencies.
Placement of British and American agencies is not comparable.

92

politico-economic systems of the United States and of Britain differ in important respects, to be sure; yet both major parties in both countries are attacking their economic problems with fundamentally the same kinds of techniques. Ideological differences between the parties in each country and between the countries themselves are significant in affecting the choice of techniques; but policy in any case is technique-minded, and it is becoming increasingly difficult in both countries to argue policy in terms of the mythical grand alternatives.

THE AREA OF AGREEMENT ON TECHNIQUES

A curious and encouraging aspect of the debate on economic policy is that ideological differences cannot disguise an emerging agreement on appropriate social techniques. John Jewkes wages furious war on the Left in his *Ordeal by Planning;* [8] but on the particulars of economic policy for Britain he is close to James Meade, a self-described liberal socialist.[9] Both would applaud much of Henry Simons' *A Positive Program for Laissez-Faire,*[10] W. Arthur Lewis' *Principles of Economic Planning,*[11] and Wilhelm Röpke's *The Social Crisis of Our Time.*[12] If conservatives, liberals, socialists, planners, and anti-planners find themselves in growing agreement the closer they press to concrete policy problems, this is a fact of extraordinary significance for the social sciences and for the possibilities of rational politico-economic action.

8. John Jewkes, *Ordeal by Planning*, The Macmillan Company, New York, 1948.

9. James E. Meade, *op. cit.*

10. Henry C. Simons, *A Positive Program for Laissez-Faire* (Public Policy Pamphlet No. 15), University of Chicago Press, Chicago, 1934.

11. W. Arthur Lewis, *op. cit.*

12. Wilhelm Röpke, *The Social Crisis of Our Time*, William Hodge and Co., London, and University of Chicago Press, Chicago, 1950.

PART TWO What Role for Government Expenditure?

The Economic Functions of the State in English Classical Political Economy

LIONEL ROBBINS

Lord Robbins is Professor of Political Economy Emeritus at the London School of Economics. The Theory of Economic Policy, in which this essay appears, is a survey of the attitudes and doctrines of classical economists toward the appropriate economic functions of government.

I DO NOT think that it is any exaggeration to suggest that to-day, apart from a handful of specialists, the great body of the educated public tends to regard the Classical conception of the functions of the state as sufficiently characterized by Carlyle's phrase, "Anarchy plus the constable", or by Lassalle's simile of the night watchman. It is this view that I propose to examine.

SPECIMENS OF EXTREME INDIVIDUALISM

Now I do not question that such conceptions of the functions of the state have been widely held. At most times, in the period under discussion, it would be easy to cull from the political discussions of the day utterances and *obiter dicta* which implied just such an attitude as is suggested by Lassalle's simile. Nor am I prepared to contend that such an attitude is only to be found in the rough-and-tumble of popular controversy. On the contrary, I am clear that it is possible to discover sentiments of this sort on the lips of men who are certainly to be described as economists or social philosophers.

Take, for instance, the alleged conversation between Mercier de La Rivière and Catherine the Great. As you may know, the French economists, the Physiocrats, had a great vogue among the enlightened despots of the eighteenth century. They were invited to the various courts; their advice was solicited by the great personages. Among those who were thus distinguished was Mercier de La Rivière, the author of *L'Ordre naturel et essentiel des sociétés politiques*, which Adam Smith thought to be the best exposition of the Physiocratic system. He was asked by Catherine the Great to visit Moscow. According to Thiebault, when he arrived, the following conversation took place:

Catherine. "Sir, can you tell me the best way to govern a state?"
Mercier de La Rivière. "There is only one way, Madame. Be just, that is to say, uphold the constitution and observe the laws."
C. "But on what basis should laws be made?"
M. "On one basis only, Your Majesty, on the nature of things and of men."
C. "Most certainly. But when one wishes to make these laws what rules should be observed?"
M. "Madame, to give laws to mankind is God's prerogative. How can mere man venture on such a task? By what right would he dictate to those whom God has not placed in his hands?"
C. "To what then do you reduce the science of government?"
M. "To study the laws which God has so manifestly engraven in human society from the time of its creation. To seek to go beyond this would be a great mistake and a disastrous undertaking."
C. "Sir, it has been a great pleasure to meet you. I wish you good day." [1]

Perhaps this an over-simplified version of what actually happened; anecdotes of courts not infrequently tend that way. But no one who has read typical specimens of the Physiocratic literature would contend that it was altogether out of character.

Or take Bastiat. In his *Harmonies économiques* he lays it down that "It is the essence of government that it acts on the citizens by way of constraint. Therefore it cannot have any other rational function but the legitimate defence of individual rights, it has no authority but to make respected the liberties and the properties

1. *Souvenirs de Berlin* (2nd edition), vol. iii, pp. 167 *seq.* I owe the quotation to Oncken, *Geschichte des Nationalökonomie*, Bd. i, p. 421.

of all. . . . Beyond justice, I challenge anyone to imagine a governmental intervention which is not an injustice. . . . Thus: to preserve the public security: to administer the common domain [Rivers, Forest, Roads], to impose taxes; here, I believe, is the rational circle within which the function of government must be circumscribed or restricted. . . ." [2]

The attitude of Herbert Spencer in *Man versus the State* is of a similar order of simplicity. Of course, the object of this famous polemic is chiefly negative: the author is arguing against a trend of policy; and it is a common habit in such circumstances to tend to overstate the case. Nevertheless, it is certainly not unfair to depict him as opposed on principle to state regulation concerning health, safety and compulsory education. The regulations themselves, he argues, are usually pernicious; and the cumulative tendency is towards the servile state.

THE CLASSICAL THEORY

Thus there can be no doubt that doctrines as extreme as those pilloried by Carlyle and Lassalle have had extensive currency and the support of famous names. But they did not have the support of the Classical Economists. To identify such doctrines with the declared and easily accessible views of the Classical Economists is a sure sign of ignorance or malice. This is a strong statement, which must be supported by extensive evidence.

According to Adam Smith, the state has three functions, "first, the duty of protecting the society from the violence and invasion of other independent societies; secondly, the duty of protecting, as far as possible, every member of the society from the injustice or oppression of every other member of it; and, thirdly, [note the wording here] the duty of erecting and maintaining certain public works and certain public institutions, which it can never be for the interest of any individual, or small number of individuals, to erect and maintain; because the profit could never repay the expense to any individual or small number of individuals, though it may frequently do much more than repay it to a great society".[3]

2. Bastiat, *Œuvres complètes* (1864), vol. vi, pp. 553–555.
3. Adam Smith, *The Wealth of Nations* (Cannan's edition), vol. ii, pp. 184–185.

Before we go any further, it is interesting to compare this formulation of the functions of the state with the formulation which we find in Keynes' celebrated pamphlet *The End of Laissez-Faire*. "The most important *Agenda* of the state", says Keynes, following Bentham's terminology, "relate not to those activities which private individuals are already fulfilling, but to those functions [please note the wording again] which fall outside the sphere of the individual, to those decisions which are made by *no one* if the State does not make them. The important thing for Government is not to do things which individuals are doing already, and to do them a little better or a little worse; but to do those things which at present are not done at all." [4]

It would, of course, be misleading to suggest that the *content* of Lord Keynes' *agenda* was identical with that of Adam Smith's —control of aggregate investment and policy designed to affect the size and quality of the population were conspicuous among his illustrations—and it is quite clear that such were alien to Adam Smith's conception. But the *formal* similarity is not an accident; it indicates the essential continuity of thought in the tradition of economic liberalism concerning the positive nature of the co-operation between the state and the individual. Nor must we regard the content of Adam Smith's *agenda* as limited to provision of roads, canals, harbours and such like utilities. He made a most powerful plea for popular education and he indicated that, had he known of any available technique, he would have favoured health legislation.[5]

For the rest, we have already seen that he laid it down as a principle that those exertions of the natural liberty of a few individuals which might endanger the whole society ought to be restrained; and a careful reading of the *Wealth of Nations* will yield a very substantial number of illustrations, from quality certificates for linen and woollen cloth [6] and regulations concerning land settlement in new countries,[7] to the control of the price of bread

4. *Supra*, pp. 46–47.

5. Adam Smith, *op. cit.* vol. ii, p. 272: ". . . It would deserve its most serious attention to prevent a leprosy or any other loathsome and offensive disease, though neither mortal nor dangerous from spreading itself. . . ."

6. *Op. cit.* vol. i, p. 124.

7. *Ibid.* vol. ii, pp. 73–74.

if the supply is in the hands of a monopoly.[8] I have no desire to present a paradoxical picture of Smith as an enlightened interventionist. That would be a false perspective. But the perspective is no less false which presents him as one who would reduce the functions of the state to those of the night watchman.

I pass next to Bentham, whose significance as providing the philosophical background for the later developments has not, I think, always been fully appreciated by historians of economic thought.

If we read the famous *Be quiet* injunction to government which is also to be found in the first chapter of the *Manual of Political Economy*, we may easily be tempted to put Bentham among the extreme exponents of a negative view of state function. Although there is an explicit presumption that, over a wide field, interference is inadvisable, there is no suggestion that it is ruled out *a priori* by some system of natural rights. Bentham had no use whatever for the *Naturrecht*, and he continually goes out of his way to make this clear. Thus he is most contemptuous about those who would argue that because taxation involves a burden on those who pay it, therefore, it should be avoided. "It would . . . be a gross error, and an extremely mischievous one, to refer to the defalcation thus resulting from the mass of liberty or free agency, as affording a conclusive objection against the inter-position of the law for this or any other purpose. Every law which does not consist in the repeal, total or partial, of a coercive law, is itself a coercive law. To reprobate as a mischief resulting from this or that law, a property which is the essence of all law, is to betray . . . a total unacquaintance with what may be called the logic of the laws." [9] According to the principle of utility, as distinct from the *Naturrecht*, the expediency of any act of government must be judged solely by its consequences and not regarded as ruled out in advance by some metaphysical system of rights. In

8. *Ibid.* vol. i, p. 144.
9. Bentham, *Manual of Political Economy:* Works (ed. Bowring), vol. iii, pp. 34, 70. "In recommending freedom of trade, I suppose the minds of merchants in their sound, that is, their ordinary state. But there have been times when they acted as though they were delirious: such were the period of the Mississippi Scheme in France and the South Sea Scheme in England. The other classes of people would have had ground for seeking to divert their fellow citizens from the purchase of the smoke sold by Law, or of the *bubbles* of the South Sea."

fact, even in the *Manual* we find the most surprising examples of state action which is said to be beneficial—from accumulation, for instance, of large stocks of food against famine in circumstances where the private market does not function adequately in this respect,[10] to intervention to prevent over-speculation in stock markets.[11] He has, moreover, Adam Smith's formal argument regarding institutions involving indiscriminate benefit, illustrated *inter alia* by a justification of the building of the Caledonian Canal which might easily come from a modern work dilating on the arcana of the doctrine of external economies—though it has not the same esoteric air.[12]

But I shall give a false impression if I restrict myself to piquant examples. You get Bentham quite out of perspective if you do not think of him essentially as the great legal inventor, the greatest perhaps in history, continually seeking all along the line to erect a structure of institutions, thought out in great detail, within which action is so limited and co-ordinated as to create the good society. I wonder how many now living have ever opened the *Constitutional Code*, the great project for a practical Utopia on which Bentham lavished so much of the care and emotion of the final years of his life. Those who do, even if they restrict themselves only to the contents table, must find a picture which squares very ill with the contemporary idea of the *laissez-faire* state. Let me quote the Bentham cabinet: besides the Prime Minister:—

> Election Minister.
> Legislation Minister.
> Army Minister.
> Navy Minister.
> Preventive Service Minister (Police, Fire, etc.).
> Interior Communication Minister.
> Indigence Relief Minister.

10. *Ibid.* p. 71.
11. *Ibid.* p. 71.
12. "The justification of the communication from sea to sea through Scotland by the Caledonian Canal, is to be sought for in the same principles, though the preponderance of profit over expense can scarcely be expected to prove equally considerable. Of the profit part, though to an unassignable amount will distribute itself among a limited, and perhaps individually assignable description of individuals: other part, in portions altogether unassignable, among individuals more clearly assignable; viz. among the community at large." *Ibid.* p. 41, note.

Education Minister.
Domain Minister.
Health Minister.
Foreign Relations Minister.
Trade Minister.
Finance Minister.[13]

Pretty comprehensive is it not? When we look into the detail of
the arrangements we note that care has been taken to provide a
Central Statistical Office ("statistic function"), a competitively
selected Civil Service, and many other administrative arrangements hardly achieved even at the present day. I confess that
when I find this sort of thing I feel that, in some respects at any
rate, modern practice has yet some little distance to go before
it catches up with Jeremy Bentham.[14]

I must not prolong unduly this procession of witnesses. But we
must not restrict ourselves to the founders: it might be argued
that there had been some departure from these standards in the
second and third generations. As is well known, Mill in his *Principles* devoted a whole book (Book V) to the province of government, which abounds in illustrations of what I am trying to
demonstrate. It might be thought that his attitude was untypical.
I prefer therefore to rely on McCulloch and Senior, of whom, on
popular estimates, less of this sort of thing is to be expected.

McCulloch has a systematic discussion of the functions of government in his *Principles*. This embraces a wide field of the kind
that we should expect in one who had read Smith and Bentham,
and includes a strong plea for the statutory limitation of the
dividends of public utility organizations. In his treatise on inheritance we may note a striking, though not untypical, repudia-
tion of the principle of *laissez-faire*. "The principle of *laissez-faire*
may be safely trusted to in some things but in many more it is
wholly inapplicable; and to appeal to it on all occasions savours
more of the policy of a parrot than of a statesman or a philosopher." [15]

Senior is even stronger. In his anonymous review of Mill in the
Edinburgh Review in 1848 he poses the question, "Is it true that
governments ought to confine themselves to affording protection

13. Bentham, *op. cit.* vol. ix, p. 7.
14. *Ibid.* p. 447.
15. J. R. McCulloch, *Treatise on the Succession to Property Vacant by
Death* (1848), p. 156.

against force and fraud?" and comes to the conclusion that the arguments in favour of this principle "cannot be supported". He even takes exception to Mill's use of the term "optional" as applied to the function of government. "Like the words 'boon' or 'concession', it seems to imply that there may be useful measures which the government of a country may at its discretion adopt or reject." [16] And in his Oxford lectures of 1847–48 he lays it down that "the only rational foundation of government, the only foundation of a right to govern and a correlative duty to obey is, expediency—the general benefit of the community. It is the duty of a government to do whatever is conducive to the welfare of the governed. The only limit to this duty is power . . . it appears to me that the most fatal of all errors would be the general admission of the proposition that a government has no right to interfere for any purpose except for that of affording protection, for such an admission would be preventing our profiting by experience, and even from acquiring it." [17]

Unless words of this sort are to be taken as deliberate deception, they must surely be regarded as conclusive evidence against the attribution to those who used them of the night-watchman theory of the functions of government.

16. J. S. Mill's *Political Economy: Edinburgh Review*, October 1848, vol. clxxviii, p. 294 *seq*.

17. This lecture has never been published in its original form. But a snippet is given in the compilation of extracts from Senior's published and unpublished works entitled *Industrial Efficiency and Social Economy* (edited S. Leon Levy), vol. ii, p. 302.

Government and the Sovereign Consumer

FRANCIS M. BATOR

Francis M. Bator is Associate Professor of Economics at the Massachusetts Institute of Technology. His book The Question of Government Spending *constructs a case for public expenditure on the ground that private enterprise cannot satisfactorily meet the whole range of consumer wants.*

Is, or is not, the consumer to be sovereign? If we believe that the objective of economic activity is to cater to the individual consumer, then, it is argued, we must abide by the allocations implied by consumers' tastes as revealed by their market choices. Absorption of resources by paternalistic activities which do not meet a market "test" is prima facie illegitimate; and, while it must be tolerated as the lesser of evils as regards provision for defense, the administration of jails, and other "obviously" public activities, any shift of resources from private to public use is to be deplored irrespective of how much you and I may prefer more public hospitals to more automobiles. Or so the argument goes.

In fact, few people believe in the doctrine of consumer sovereignty in its pure, unadulterated form. But what if everyone did? What if we could all agree that consumers' preferences are the only admissible touchstone for economic performance—that we will suppress any qualms about attributing ultimate significance to people's television-bombarded tastes for appliances (and disregard all difficulties with children and the insane and all problems of technical ignorance)? Would it follow that there is no need for allocating resources through political decision? Or does the very doctrine of consumer sovereignty impose on government, aside from its income distribution, stabilization, and general policing functions, an obligation partially to short-circuit market processes in the allocation of resources? [1]

---

1. Even if the answer were in the negative—if there were no narrowly "economic" case for allocation by government—one could not rule out preference for modes of organization other than laissez-faire markets on quite different grounds. A fastidious humanitarian, for instance, might

102

A DIGRESSION ON MARKET EFFICIENCY

The negative contention—that there is no call for allocation by government—stands or falls with the crucial premise of the laissez-faire position, notably that a price-market system is such an efficient instrument for inducing consumers to reveal their preferences and producers to cater to these that allocations not subjected to a market test are bound to do worse by consumers than allocations which pass such a test. Is this so with regard to all activities? What is there of truth and error in the notion of market efficiency? [2]

The full answer, as it has emerged during the course of a century and a half of polemics and careful analysis, is unavoidably technical, being based on perhaps the most subtle insights of modern economic theory.[3] Yet its essence is simple enough. Imagine a world (1) where each individual's market choices reflect a subjective *preference ordering* which permits him to register

---

argue that to organize society so as to take advantage of man's instinct for material self-aggrandizement is bound to demean the human spirit and hence is immoral, no matter how much more efficient such organization may be in catering to "standard of living" values. On the other hand, a European-type liberal may hold that a variety of political and social non-output values relating to the configuration of power, opportunity, etc., are so much better served by some form of even grossly inefficient market institutions than by possible alternative modes of more efficient organization as to warrant choice of the former. But these are different matters; here my concern is with a price-market system not as an end, nor even as a means to noneconomic political and ethical ends, but simply as an organizational device for catering to consumers' wants. In particular, I am not concerned with the right "freely" to choose in markets.

2. In the notion, to take a significant recent formulation, that "when it comes to the advancing and expanding of our economy, that is by and large the business of Americans; the federal government can help, but . . . *our federal money will never be spent so intelligently and in so useful a fashion for the economy as will the expenditures that would be made by the private citizen, the taxpayer, if he hadn't had so much of it funneled off into the Federal Government.*" (President Eisenhower, January 14, 1959, cited in Transcript of News Conference, *New York Times,* January 15, 1959, p. 18; my italics.)

3. And on a line of thought that goes back to Adam Smith, Ricardo, Mill, Walras, and Marshall. Important modern contributions have been made by Vilfredo Pareto, Enrico Barone, Knut Wicksell, and Professor A. C. Pigou, all writing just before World War I, and more recently by Abram Bergson, A. P. Lerner, and Paul Samuelson, and by H. Hotelling, J. R. Hicks, and Oscar Lange. For a detailed technical exposition, see my "The Simple Analytics of Welfare Maximization," *American Economic Review,* March 1957, pp 22–59. [For a simpler exposition see, for example, P. A. Samuelson, *Economics,* 5th edition (New York: McGraw-Hill, 1961),

preference or indifference as between any two bundles of goods and services independently of any other person's choices; (2) where the input-output decisions of each producer—his decisions about how much labor and raw material to buy, what machines to use, how much of what to produce, etc.—reflect a single-minded urge to maximize profit, subject only to the state of the production arts and market prices; and (3) where there exist very many independent buyers and sellers in every market, and hence a state of perfect competition. It can be shown that in such a world the particular allocation and distribution of scarce resources brought about by the separate decisions of millions of profit-maximizing producers and by the consumption and leisure-work decisions of millions of consumers, all facing competitively determined prices in every market, will tend to be *efficient.* In what sense? In the very special sense that there will remain no possible reallocations, no shifts in inputs, outputs, and in distribution *such as would make some one or more individuals better off in terms of their own preferences without making some other individuals worse off in terms of theirs. . . .*

[Given these assumptions] about the independence of preferences and the feasibility of perfect competition, markets will yield efficient solutions. Each producer, concerned only with his own profit, and each consumer, bent on getting the most out of what he has, will do precisely what is needed to exhaust all mutually advantageous reallocations. Just this, in fact, is the sum and substance of Adam Smith's famed theorem of the "invisible hand." [4]

It would not be appropriate here—sadly, because it is a thing of beauty—to set out in detail the analytical content of the theorem. Its kernel lies in the remarkable fact that the mathematics of solving the problem of efficiency makes use of a set of auxiliary variables ("unknowns") *which turn out to have all the earmarks of prices, wage rates, interest rates, and rents.* This in the double sense that (1) the computational procedure involved in finding an efficient combination of inputs, outputs, and distribution hap-

---

pp.608–9, 678–89; also, Oscar Lange and F. M. Taylor, *On the Economic Theory of Socialism* (Minneapolis: University of Minnesota, 1938), pp. 57–90. *Editor.*]

4. In precise technical language, the theorem asserts that the equilibrium conditions which characterize a system of perfectly competitive markets will, given our assumptions, exactly correspond to the conditions implied by the solution of the mathematical maximizing problem which defines efficiency.

pens to yield, as a by-product, numerical magnitudes for these auxiliary variables which correspond precisely to the prices on which competitive markets would settle to cause supply to match demand in every market; and (2) that profit- and preference-maximizing decisions by millions of producers and consumers, all responding to these price numbers, would yield just that pattern of inputs, outputs, and distribution which the mathematical solution of the efficiency problem calls for. What this implies is that the rules followed, e.g., by competing producers bent on maximizing their own profits, are precisely the rules they must follow if allocation is to be efficient. *Example:* a profit-eager producer facing competitively determined prices will increase his output up to where the increase in total cost due to the last unit. i.e., *marginal cost,* just equals the increase in revenue he can get by selling the last unit, i.e., price. But marginal-cost-equal-to-price can be shown to be just the rule producers *must* follow if their input-output decisions are to lead to efficient allocation.

WHAT ROLE FOR GOVERNMENT SPENDING?

If a price-market "game" is a flawlessly efficient computing device with a more or less workable institutional counterpart, what sense is there in bypassing markets? [The question we ask is whether there is] a case for government spending even in a world of single-minded and error-free profit- and preference-maximizing calculations, where consumers' tastes are really all that count.

Transfer Payments [5] · How are dollar votes to be distributed among people? The ethical postulate that we should do as well as possible by consumers' tastes provides no answer. It is neutral as among the *infinite* number of efficient solutions, which range from all food and all clothing going to Crusoe to where everything goes to Friday.

Choice among efficient combinations involves ultimate ethical values (call them "equity values"), and it would be sheer accident if the particular efficient configuration generated by markets turned out to rate higher in terms of my ethical valuations, or yours, or Thomas Jefferson's, or that of a politically engineered

5. Recall that transfer payments redistribute income but do not constitute a claim on resources.

"consensus," than all other efficient, and even many inefficient, solutions. It is evidently not true that to secure the efficiency vouchsafed by competitive markets we must accept the distribution of income generated by such markets. It is possible to break the link between ownership and "final" income distribution by means of tax-financed interpersonal "transfers" and to do so without exempting any allocations from a private market test. In fact, this is precisely what is done. Government spending on old-age assistance, on veterans' cash bonuses, and the like does not cause resources to bypass markets; it simply redistributes command over resources among people. The final spending for goods and services is by private individuals bidding in markets, guided by their personal preferences.[6]

Exhaustive Expenditure and Subsidies · The case for or against pure transfer expenditure cannot be resolved, it appears, by invoking the doctrine of consumer sovereignty; explicit attention must be given to the ethics and politics of income distribution. But what about government purchases of goods and services and subsidies? Is there any justification, in terms of the principle of efficiently catering to consumers' tastes, for bypassing a market test and allocating some resources via political procedures?[7]

The answer hangs on the validity of the assumptions about preferences and conditions of production which are necessary for the "invisible hand" theorem to hold. In the above discussion of market efficiency, these assumptions, while repeatedly mentioned, were treated rather lightly. Yet it is the failure of the assumptions even approximately to match the facts of the real world that constitutes the core of the strictly "economic" case for

6. It is a different matter that some hold any such redistribution wrong on *ethical* grounds, as violating the "natural right" of everyone to his property, or to what he earns, or to what he is "worth" on the market. To ascribe ethical significance to the particular distribution of income effected by markets is to introduce a value judgment over and above the value of efficiently catering to consumers' tastes.

7. Or, in the case of subsidies, of modifying the effect of the market test? [In a later paragraph, Bator states, "With direct interaction of preferences, decentralization of allocation decisions via flawlessly competitive markets can no longer be assumed costless; private decisions will waste opportunities for making some people better off without hurting others." This condition, which Bator assumes away for the sake of argument, would justify government subsidies and possibly expenditures. *Editor.*]

public spending.[8] If we care about consumers' preferences, we must cope with two related technical characteristics of the real world which cause decentralized market calculation to be grossly inefficient—economies of scale in production, and the prevalence of what the economist calls "public goods."

Where the "Invisible Hand" Fails (1) · Competition requires that there be "very many" producers in every market. If economies of large-scale production confer a cost advantage on firms that are large relative to the total market, a few technically efficient producers will saturate the market, and competition, in the technical sense, will break down. Each producer will be large enough for his *own* output decisions to have an appreciable effect on price. This in turn will cause the profit-minded producer to fix his output at a level where marginal cost is less than price, i.e., at a level lower than is required for efficient allocation. Output will fall short of where the extra cost to society is just covered by extra benefit as measured by price.[9]

Nor can antitrust action, no matter how ideally designed, cor-

8. That such an "economic" case is too narrow a foundation for even an "economic" theory of government is almost too obvious to warrant comment. Indeed, some may feel that to explore what justification there may be for government spending in terms of the ethical postulates of Manchester liberalism is a foolish waste of time, especially since it requires that we take a rather abstract view of markets. Yet quite apart from the analytical insight the exercise may offer, it is not clear to me that the "Manchester view" either is, or indeed that it ought to be, so dead as to warrant the charge of irrelevance.

9. The technical reason is simple enough. While, for *efficient* allocation, output should be increased up to where the extra cost of the last unit just equals the *price* people are willing to pay, the producer is interested in the balance between extra cost and extra (i.e., *marginal*) revenue. In a competitive market where, to take an example, an increase in a single farmer's output will not appreciably reduce the price of wheat, the extra revenue that accrues to the farmer if he sells an extra bushel is just equal to the price. But where a single producer is large enough relative to the market to take account of the effect on price of changes in his *own* output, his marginal revenue will no longer equal price. Marginal revenue on, say, the 101st unit of output will equal, rather, the price on the 101st unit *less* the reduction in revenue (i.e., the sales value) on the first 100 units due to the drop in market price which is caused by throwing the 101st unit on the market. Hence at the level of output at which the producer's total profit is at a maximum, i.e., where the extra revenue due to the last unit is just equal to the extra cost, such extra (marginal) cost will be less than price. People would be willing to pay more for an additional unit of output than the extra cost involved in producing it.

rect the situation. While useful in controlling or eliminating concentration of market power which is based on other than technical or administrative economies of large-scale production (e.g., concentration based on financial advantages of size due to imperfections in capital markets), trying to maintain many small units if there are true resource economies to be had by large-scale production is obviously a self-defeating procedure.[10]

Price regulation of the right sort, as approximated by the best public utility commissions, is more akin to what is needed. A publicly administered price, if it allows for positive profit, will induce as-if competitive behavior. For maximum profit, output will be increased up to where marginal cost is just covered by the centrally fixed price. But even this fails to get at the heart of the matter. It fails, notably, to take account of the curious fact that the price-output combination required for efficient allocation may well imply negative profits, i.e., continuing losses.

The key to this paradox lies in the meaning of "economies of scale." The existence of scale economies at a given level of output means no more nor less than that a small increase in output from that level will cause unit cost (cost per unit: total cost divided by output) to fall. It happens, moreover, that at such a point of declining *unit* cost, marginal cost: the increment in total cost due to an extra unit of output, is necessarily less than unit cost.[11] Yet it is generally still true that, if allocation is to be efficient, output must be increased up to where marginal cost is just covered by price. But if price is to equal marginal cost where marginal cost is less than unit cost, price must be less than unit cost. Evidently efficiency requires that producers operating in a

10. This is not to gainsay that antitrust measures can reduce some of the undesirable effects of concentration. But their proper role is not to try to maintain the world as it would be if perfect competition were feasible. Rather, it is to serve as one of a variety of complementary instruments of social control appropriate to a world where perfect competition is not feasible.

11. In fact, it is the difference between *marginal* cost and *unit* cost that causes unit cost to fall as output is increased. If unit cost were $1.00 and marginal cost $1.00, why should unit cost fall? The increase in total cost due to an extra unit of output would be $1.00 and unit cost, i.e., total cost divided by output, would remain $1.00. But if unit cost at an output of 20 units is $1.00, while the increase in total cost due to the 21st unit is only $.50, the unit cost of 21 units would be $\dfrac{20 \times \$1 + 1 \times \$.50}{21} = \dfrac{\$20.50}{21}$, or less than $1.00.

range of decreasing cost operate at a loss. Evidently, also, no profit-seeking producer will long do so.[12]

Consider, for example, the "production" of bridge crossings. Assume, to take an extreme instance, that once the bridge in question is built, all wear and tear is a function of time rather than use, i.e., that there are no additional costs associated with extra crossings. (The bridge is never so full as to give rise to crowding.) The marginal cost to society, in terms of scarce resources, of an additional crossing is zero. It follows—the proposition is mathematically demonstrable, as well as, in this case, intuitively obvious—that the efficient ration price for a crossing is precisely zero. A positive price such as would discourage even a single crossing would cause allocation to be inefficient; there would remain unexploited a costless crossing which could make someone better off without hurting anyone else. Yet it is equally evident that charging a price of zero for crossings will hardly raise sufficient revenue to cover the cost of building the bridge.

It is tempting to argue that if this is the case, if the bridge cannot pay for itself, then it should not be built. But this is not even plausible. It implies that no facility with a large fixed (initial) cost and relatively low *variable* cost (and therefore low marginal cost) should ever be built. (It is just such high fixed-cost and low variable-cost facilities that are characterized by unit costs which decline with output; it is simply a matter of spreading the "fixed" overhead.) Not only bridges but also roads, railroads, airfields, dams, ports, would all be ruled out as uneconomic. But of course the proposition is indefensible. It is easy to prove that where technology gives rise to economies of scale at the relevant levels of output, profitability at a competitive price is not a necessary condition of efficiency. The test of profit breaks down.[13]

12. Where market imperfections are pervasive, there are also other difficulties with the rule that output be increased to where marginal cost equals price. If one is trying to get nine drunks who are tied to each other to walk in a straight line, it may not help to sober up one of them.

13. To a sophisticated businessman used to running a decentralized multi-division firm all this would not come as too much of a surprise. Not every process in a well-run firm should be expected to cover its cost in terms of the right set of internal accounting prices. *Total* profit is the deciding criterion, and it may be worth while for a firm to build a private bridge between its two installations on opposite sides of a river yet charge a zero accounting price for its use by the various decentralized manufacturing and administrative divisions. (Zero would certainly be the right price if a positive accounting price discouraged the use of the bridge while extra use involved no extra cost.) The bridge considered as a separate

Nor, by the way, is monopoly a satisfactory way out. It is true that in many cases where competition is unworkable—where one or a few firms are bound by reason of scale efficiency to saturate the market—monopolists or a few large oligopolists, so-called, could all make a profit. It may well be, for instance, that there is a positive price at which the operation of our bridge would be profitable, i.e., would more than cover cost. It may even be that such private monopolistic operation is the best of the administratively and politically feasible organizational devices for getting the bridge built and operated. But the fact remains that any such noncompetitive rationing of crossings by a price calculated to maximize net revenue results in less-than-efficient allocation. Bridge crossings would be restricted below the number which would just equate the cost of the last crossing to offer-price. In our example, where marginal cost is zero, some socially *costless* crossings would be discouraged. The output of crossings could be increased without decreasing the output of anything else.[14]

Monopoly, moreover, may not even be a second-best answer, not even with appropriate "discipline" imposed by public agencies staffed by administrators straight out of Plato. It is entirely possible wherever economies of scale are substantial that there is no price which would cover the cost of a facility which nevertheless is required for efficient allocation. It is an old but still intriguing proposition of economics that an activity may be necessary for efficiency though even monopoly operation would fail to cover its cost. The only true test is provided by a perfectly "discriminating" monopolist, so called, who manages for every single crossing to squeeze out of every single customer the maximum toll that the individual is prepared to pay to be permitted that one crossing. The resources that go into a bridge can be shown to be misallocated only if such a perfectly discriminating monopolist, who confronts every user at every crossing with a lump-sum, take-it-or-leave-it offer which reflects a perfect assessment of the customer's desire for that crossing, should fail to cover the cost of the bridge.[15]

The moral of all this is plain. As regards activities characterized

activity would make accounting losses, yet total company profits would be increased.

14. Note that the effect on allocation is quite distinct from what usually worries people about monopoly—its effect on income distribution.

15. Put differently, there exist many situations where no single "admission" price would raise sufficient revenue to cover the cost of an establishment,

by economies of large-scale production (at levels of output which are relevant in terms of the volume of demand), a price-market system, while it may still serve to raise revenue to cover cost, will no longer be simultaneously efficient in rationing output. Alternatively, the price which will efficiently ration output will fail to raise sufficient revenue to avoid loss. Monopolistic operation (at price greater than marginal cost) may or may not succeed in covering cost; where so, however, there will be inefficient curtailment of output. And where not, subsidy may be unavoidable if there is to be any output whatever.

This is the sum and substance of the *qualitative* case, in terms of efficiency, against exclusive reliance on the test of profit as concerns such things as railroads, airlines, roads, public parks, public libraries, river-valley development, and perhaps even the postal services. All these activities are characterized by decreasing unit cost at the relevant levels of output. Competition, in the economist's sense, is not feasible. In some cases monopolistic operation may yield a "full-cost" price, but, since by the very nature of the situation a price which covers unit cost will exceed marginal cost, the result is misallocation. In other cases, there exists no full-cost price, i.e., no price which will yield enough revenue to cover cost, and it is impossible to get any output without subsidy (barring, perhaps, only a very sophisticated structure of differential prices). If we take seriously the case for efficiently catering to consumers' preferences, unadulterated markets will not do.[16]

Where the "Invisible Hand" Fails (2) · Where marginal cost is positive but less than unit cost, efficient allocation (in an ideal world) requires that output be rationed by a price equal to

e.g., of a repertory theater company where, however, lump-sum contributions based on an "all plays free or no theater" choice, would, if only people could be made honestly to own up to their preferences, amply cover cost. (The qualification about "owning up" has to do with the problem of "publicness" discussed in the next section.)

16. It does not follow, of course, that we should give up on market mediation in *all* or even most sectors of the economy where decreasing-cost activities predominate. Inefficient markets may often do much better than any feasible alternative mode of organization. (To cite only one reason, subsidies require taxes, which in turn give rise to inefficiency.) The point is only that we cannot count on market decisions to lead to even approximately efficient allocation when it comes to strongly decreasing-cost activities; that to allocate resources to such activities according to their commercial profitability may be exceedingly costly.

marginal cost and that the resulting losses be subsidized. This is typically the situation in so-called public utilities. Additional use entails some additional cost, but the initial fixed cost of the facility, whether it be a port, a dam, a thermal station, or a railroad line, is so high relative to costs which vary with the rate at which the facility is used that unit cost declines with output, and equality of price and marginal cost implies operating in the red.

There are activities, however, where the additional cost of extra use is literally zero. The economist labels the output of such activities "public." A good or service is defined as public if X's consumption of it leads to no subtraction from what is left over for consumption by Y and Z. Radio programs, the services rendered by the beacon atop the Statue of Liberty, the protection provided by the Strategic Air Command are some examples. The additional resource costs of an extra TV viewer, of an extra listener at an uncrowded open air concert, of an additional child watching a fireworks display, of a newly naturalized citizen benefiting from the deterrent-potential of the "Nautilus," of the "Queen Mary" as well as the "Liberté" taking directional guidance from a lighthouse beacon—all are zero. Hence, for efficient allocation, price too must be zero. Pay television may be judged preferable to having to listen to toothpaste advertisements every fifteen minutes, but if it involves charging anyone a positive price for doing something that does not cost anyone else a penny, i.e., for tuning-in, it leads to inefficient allocation (though perhaps less so than does the advertising).[17]

Examples of *pure* public goods are few. Most things, even battleships and certainly open-air concerts and schools (though *not* knowledge), have an "if-more-for-you-then-less-for-me" quality. But this is of little comfort. If a commodity or a service has even a trace of "publicness," be it only in the form of by-product effects

17. Again, the proposition that price must be zero is not a dictum based on intuition but a theorem subject to formal proof. And again, it is subject to the qualification that it *may* in some instances be less inefficient to use the price system to raise the revenue required to cover the cost of a facility than to use taxes (even though this implies charging a positive price that will cause misallocation). But commercial profitability is a very poor indicator of whether a facility whose services are "public" in the technical sense is worth having to start off with. (If the assertion that the theorem about zero price is subject to proof seems puzzling, recall that allocation was defined as efficient if the configuration of inputs, outputs, and distribution corresponds exactly to the solution of a mathematical maximum problem with given constraints.)

which impinge inseparably on many people, then profit- and preference-seeking market calculation will not efficiently mediate its production and distribution. Hence the obvious fact that such things as urban renewal, hospital facilities, education, research, street lighting, vaccination programs, parks, police protection, and the like yield benefits of a "more-for-you-means-no-less-for-me" sort guarantees that market decisions with regard to these activities will fail to do justice to consumers' tastes.

It is sometimes alleged, mistakenly, that the nub of the difficulty lies in the "inability" of a producer of a public good physically to exclude users or to control the rationing of his produce among them, i.e., with "divorce of scarcity from effective ownership." The implication is that if only it weren't impossible, clumsy, costly, or illegal to "keep book" on who produces and who gets what and to enforce payment, all would be well. It is evident that for pure public goods this is not so. It is entirely *feasible* to "own" a bridge, and perhaps profitably to ration crossings; indeed, a private owner would do so. But, as was emphasized above, such profitable rationing, such "compensation" for services rendered, would inefficiently misallocate the output of bridge crossings. If in terms of alternative opportunities the extra cost of an additional crossing is zero, the only price consistent with efficiency is, once again, zero. Ditto for, say, TV programs or that most valuable of assets, new knowledge.[18]

In a sense, as use of the bridge as an example has already implied, a "public good" situation is simply a polar instance of decreasing costs. Yet it leads more directly to the core of the case

18. It would not be impossible, after all, by strengthening patent and copyright protection, to increase substantially the power of the originator to appropriate, i.e., to cash in on, the benefits of a valuable idea. (TV shows, in turn, and also radar-equipped lighthouses, could be protected from free-riders by means of electronic "scramblers.") But it is the essence of public goods that reward by ration price would be inefficient. To be efficient in rationing scarcities the price system must fail in its rewards; and if it is used to reward, it will reward the wrong things.

There are, of course, situations where exclusion is *the* binding consideration, where certain "goods" or "bads" with determinate and "profitable" efficiency prices are not (easily) appropriated. The cost to a producer of training a laborer is a case in point. The social benefit accrues over the working lifetime of the trainee; the private benefit to the producer accrues until the man quits to go to work for a competitor. The "fault" lies in the Emancipation Proclamation and in such imperfections of the capital market as make it difficult for the trainee to borrow in order to invest in himself at rates appropriate to a reasonable estimate of risk and expected return.

for tax-financed government spending than does the ordinary decreasing-cost model. The latter tends to draw one's attention to the problem of motivating producers to produce something the ration price of which, to be efficient, must be less than unit cost. This certainly requires subsidies, but why coercive, mandatory taxation? Why cannot everybody be counted on to contribute according to his anticipation of subjective, own-taste-determined benefit? Moreover, would not the sum raised by such voluntary contributions accurately reflect people's tastes for, say, a mosquito-control program, and hence provide us with just the measure of consumer benefit we need to match against the cost?

Unfortunately, the very condition which gives rise to the need for a subsidy will cause a system of voluntary contributions to misrepresent people's tastes for public goods. Sharing of *private* goods in proportion to voluntary "contributions"—which is precisely what happens where goods are rationed by price in competitive markets—is efficient because a "sensible" economic man's "contributions," his dollar purchases, accurately reflect his preference ordering. He contributes to the financing of apple production, that is, he buys apples, until the last nickel spent on apples yields just enough apples to compensate him for forgoing five cents' worth of nuts and pipe cleaners. He so "reveals" his tastes, however, only because to get apples he must pay for them, because apples will be available to him for consumption in proportion to what he spends. If apples were like firework displays, or mosquito-control programs, or open-air concerts on the neighbor's lawn, in other words, if his consumption of apples were a function not of how many he paid for but of their *total* supply, then his dollar contribution or purchase would hardly reflect his true tastes. Especially if he is one of many, he would be tempted to "understate" his desire for such "apples," i.e., for public goods, in the hope that other people would shoulder a higher share of the cost without his forgoing any of the benefit. Or conceivably, if he is one of a few and if the total cost of the facility relative to his pocketbook is small, he might underestimate others' eagerness and "overpay," ending up, and unnecessarily so, with more of public and less of private goods than he would like. But whether he underpays or overpays—and as regards costly activities (e.g., national defense) the latter is unlikely—the poker-like bluffing and dissimulation intrinsic to the problem of sharing the cost of public goods will cause not only simple allocation by price but also more elaborate systems of financing by voluntary contribution to be grossly unreliable in fixing the balance between public and private goods. It would always be possible, by changing the balance, to do what would never be feasible in a frictionless free-market world of pure private goods—make everyone better off.

We need not pursue the fine detail.[19] The point is clear enough—public good and decreasing cost phenomena cause private market decisions to go wrong. Market prices will fail to approximate true scarcity values in terms of wants; they will be loaded with misinformation, and producers' profit calculations will leave out of account much of the private benefit associated with public goods. The "invisible hand" will fumble: people's decentralized market choices will not efficiently cater to their tastes. If tastes matter, the community must take communal responsibility for the balance between private and public goods. The proposition that government has a significant allocating function turns out to be a corollary of the doctrine of consumer sovereignty.[20]

HOW PUBLIC MONEY IS SPENT

Much of the above would be beside the point if publicly financed activities did not exhibit a strong public quality. It happens, however, that fact and reason suggest otherwise—that the bulk of federal as well as state and local purchases in 1957, for instance, were for services with a strong decreasing-cost public-good quality. *Without implying anything whatever about the detailed project complexion of the various major programs, or*

19. Anyone interested should consult Paul Samuelson's originating development of the theory of public goods in the *Review of Economics and Statistics* (November 1954, 1955, and 1958).

20. The fact that people's market choices do badly by their *own* tastes is a paradox only in a trivial sense. If one adopts the useful fiction of "rationality"—as I have done throughout—a man will by definition so choose as to do the best by his own tastes, *given the environment* (i.e., prices). But he will do so whether the ratio of the price of Cadillacs to the price of lollypops is thirty thousand to one or one to thirty thousand. If the latter price ratio prevailed he would still do the best he could, but since the real opportunity cost of Cadillacs is in fact much greater than that of lollypops, market choices would hardly do well by tastes. If it is the right to choose that matters, any set of prices invented by an O.P.A. man gone berserk would do as well as any other.

For a technical discussion of the various modes and causes of market failure, see my "The Anatomy of Market Failure," *Quarterly Journal of Economics*, August 1958, pp. 351–379.

about the merits of the organizational devices being used, or, most emphatically, about the appropriate quantitative scale of such programs, it is evident that it cannot simply be assumed that market mediation would have done better by people's wants than did public allocation as regards national defense; general government; international affairs and finance; public health and sanitation; education; police, fire-protection, and prisons; regulation of commerce and finance; highway, water, and air transportation; transit, electricity, water, gas, and postal services; and conservation, development, and recreational use of natural resources. In 1957 these categories accounted for 96.8 per cent of public purchases of goods and services [hereafter denoted "G"].

About the other 3.2 per cent ($2.81 billion) of G, horseback judgment is more difficult even in gross qualitative terms, especially since most of the money was used to support programs the primary purpose of which is to provide income compensation to particular groups of people (i.e., to redistribute income). Expenditure on veterans' hospitals and medical care ($813 million, all federal) and on veterans' education and training ($9 million) is clearly of this sort, yet it can perhaps be defended in terms of the public quality of the services rendered. Equivalent cash disbursements to veterans would not have resulted in equivalent allocations to hospital facilities even if veterans' own preferences had called for such allocations. The same is true of the $185 million (all but $9 million of it state-local) that was spent on housing and community redevelopment.[21] On the other hand, the $895 million of G-type expenditure on public assistance and relief and on old-age retirement benefits, etc. (most of it federal-financed state-local spending) is best defended—if it is to be defended—on grounds of income distribution. Preference for services in kind over outright cash grants cannot easily be justified except in paternalistic terms.[22]

21. Housing expenditure yields output that is partially public because people care about the physical character of the neighborhood they and their children's schoolmates live in, and hence at least some of the benefit accrues inseparably to many people.

Some of the $299 million spent on "labor and manpower" (mostly federal-grant-financed state-local G) is also of this sort. It is used in part to cover the cost of administering unemployment compensation and employment service activities, to finance the Bureau of Apprenticeship and Training, etc.

22. It does not follow, however, that it cannot be justified. Few people seriously believe that the world would be a better place if literally *all*

This leaves unaccounted-for $261 million of (net) purchases of goods and services under the "agriculture" rubric and $3.14 billion of federal spending which the Commerce Department labels "subsidies less current surplus of government enterprises." [23] Of this last, $176 million went for highways and water- and air-transport, $9 million for housing and community redevelopment, and $545 million for the postal services—all activities which would fare badly if left to markets. The bulk of the money, however—$2.73 billion of subsidies and the $261 million of G—was accounted for by agriculture, with $2.48 billion going to stabilize farm prices and income.[24] For this, of all major programs, the public-good argument contains no defense. Income maintenance is the prime consideration, and it is a sad commentary on our politics that we have been unable to agree on a less devious and less wasteful means to achieve the desired end.[25]

Agriculture aside, then, free markets would not do well by most of the major functions now served by government. The rule that allocation by markets cannot be improved upon, that shifting of resources from government to private use will necessarily improve allocation, is—or ought to be—dead.

---

paternalistic measures designed to protect people against themselves were scrapped.

23. Plus some $352 million of miscellaneous administrative expenditure labeled as "other," most of it in two categories: veterans' services, and commerce and housing. Incidentally, the percentages are relative to G gross of the $422 million of government sales.

24. Total subsidies exceeded $3.14 billion by the amount of profits earned by federal enterprises.

25. Whether or not the end is justified is a matter of distributional ethics and not economic efficiency. (Ends and means do, of course, interact. The principal reason why we have not been able to work out a less wasteful stabilization program is that people disagree over the proper objectives of such a program. In particular, the major beneficiaries of the present program are quite aware that they cannot possibly gain political acceptance for an equally lucrative but more efficient arrangement such as would identify income redistribution from taxpayers in general to particular people who are now farmers as the objective of the program. And so far, the farm bloc has had enough political power to veto any change that would really hurt.)

Gross G for agriculture was $805 million. Some of this, however, was probably for more or less public activities, e.g., for research, genuine conservation, electrification, etc.

Prices *vs.* Taxes: A Classification of U.S. Public Expenditures

O. H. Brownlee is Professor of Economics at the University of Minnesota. His contribution to a conference of the National Bureau of Economic Research on public finance addresses the question of the extent to which government services can be sold rather than financed by taxes.

ALTHOUGH I favor using price as a rationing device wherever a reasonable opportunity exists, I believe that the appropriate area for application of market pricing to the determination of how much of various goods and services government should produce is a relatively small one. Opportunities undoubtedly exist for financing such items as fire and police protection partially on the basis of service actually rendered. Nevertheless, such cases would be relatively insignificant in terms of the over-all pattern of public expenditure. I see few *major* services that ought to be financed exclusively from sales revenue that are not already being financed in this way. However, charges at less than cost might well be established for some services that are now provided free.

My criteria for evaluating whether a service is being rationed appropriately and whether the amount produced is optimal do not include the effects upon the distribution of income. If agreement could be reached with respect to how various income distributions should be ordered, the best one could be achieved independently of the production pattern of government services.

A virtue of rationing services by the price mechanism is that such a procedure permits obtaining information regarding how users value these services relative to other things that they might obtain. Together with appropriate cost information, such demand data would permit one to determine whether too little or too much of a service was being produced. For services which have no external economies or diseconomies in consumption or production, i.e., the consumption level of one person does not enter

118

directly as a variable in the utility functions of other persons and the production level does not affect the physical productivities of resources in other uses, setting the price equal to marginal production cost and noting whether there is excess demand or excess supply can, under certain conditions, tell one whether too little or too much is being produced—provided, of course, that the optimal level of output is not zero. If there are external economies or diseconomies in production or consumption, services still might be allocated by the price mechanism, but the optimal amount to produce would not be that at which price is equal to marginal cost.

The validity of these assertions and the conditions which must prevail in order for them to be used as the basis for good rules to guide resource allocation are well known. I will not reproduce the "proofs" here. Instead let me try to indicate their applicability to determining which services should be "priced" and how the resulting pattern might compare with the existing one.

CLASSIFYING PUBLIC EXPENDITURES

Among the goods and services that should not be priced are those currently labeled by economists as "public" or "community" goods, i.e., those which can be consumed by one person without a reduction in the quantities available to others.[1] "Voluntary" contributions for the support of such activities will not necessarily be sufficient to obtain the best amounts of them, since there seems to be no reasonable way of inducing persons to reveal their true preferences for such goods relative to others. Although there is no unanimity with respect to which services fall in this class, expenditures for defense and associated activities fit this classification and bulk large in the over-all expenditure pattern.

At the other pole is the class of services produced under conditions of constant or increasing marginal production cost and of a character such that there are neither external economies

1. Paul A. Samuelson, "The Pure Theory of Public Expenditures," *The Review of Economics and Statistics,* November 1954, pp. 387–9; Stephen Enke, "More on the Misuse of Mathematics in Economics: Rejoinder," *ibid.,* May 1955, pp. 131–3; Julius Margolis, "A Comment on the Pure Theory of Public Expenditure," *ibid.,* November 1955, pp. 347–9; Samuelson, "Diagramatic Exposition of a Theory of Public Expenditure," *ibid.,* November 1955, pp. 350–6; Samuelson, "Aspects of Public Expenditure Theories," *ibid.,* November 1958, pp. 332–8.

nor diseconomies of production or consumption associated with them. These should be rationed by price (or a mechanism comparable to the price mechanism), and the output at which the market clears when price is equal to marginal cost is the appropriate one to produce. For the most part, such services are not produced by government except in cases where the cost of collecting from users in accordance with quantities used is high relative to production costs. However, there is no inherent reason why government should not produce such goods providing that it attaches appropriate values to the resources that are used in production, allows for the restrictions that it imposes upon private producers in determining costs *and* does not cover losses from general tax revenues. That one or more of these conditions would be violated is not unlikely.

In between these two extremes are those services which have external economies in consumption and/or decreasing marginal production costs leading inherently to monopoly. Those with pronounced external economies in consumption generally have been produced by government; those with obvious increasing returns generally have been subject to regulation.

A detailed description of governmental services which can be classified accurately according to the three categories suggested— "public goods," services with pronounced external economies in consumption and/or production, and services which should be priced at marginal cost—is not readily available. However, a cursory examination of aggregate data suggests the following somewhat crude allocation of some of the major service categories [in the accompanying table].

The above classification is somewhat arbitrary and does not reveal the things that are of interest in determining whether services are being produced in appropriate quantities. Although it is a picture for only one short period of time, this picture is not an atypical one. Of particular interest is that (1) there are no "sales receipts" from services that benefit both the users and other parties (i.e., have pronounced external economies in consumption)—although some such receipts probably should be attributed to sanitation—and (2) there is a substantial amount of support from general tax funds for a service that I have classified as one that should be sold at marginal cost—higher education. Included in the expenditures for this service are those for research, so that all of the difference between expenditures and receipts should not

Categories of Government Service [a]

	Expenditure (billions of dollars)	"Sales Receipts" (billions of dollars)
A. "Public goods"		
1. Federal government		
a. General government	1.7	
b. National defense, including atomic energy, USIS, mutual security, State Department, and research and development	48.6	
c. Health, hospitals and medical (largely veterans)	2.4	
2. State and local governments		
a. General control	1.7	
b. Public safety [b]		
(I) Police	1.5	
(II) Fire	0.8	
c. Health, hospitals and welfare		
(I) Welfare	3.4	
(II) Hospitals [b]	3.2	
B. Services with pronounced external economies		
1. State and local governments		
a. Elementary and secondary education	11.9	
b. Sanitation		
(I) Sewage	0.9	
(II) Other sanitation	0.5	
C. Saleable services		
1. Federal government		
a. Postal service	4.1	4.0
b. General aids to business	0.2	
c. Higher education	0.45 [c]	
d. Highways		1.0
2. State and local governments		
a. Higher education	1.5	0.4
b. Highways	7.8 [d]	4.0 [c]
c. Public utilities	3.5	2.9
d. Liquor stores	0.9	1.1

[a] Data for the federal government are for 1960, and are from Executive Office of the President, *The Federal Budget in Brief*, Fiscal Year 1960. Those for state and local governments are for 1957 and are from *State and Local Government Finances in 1957*, Bureau of the Census, February, 1957.

[b] Police and fire protection as well as hospitals contain a component that is clearly not in the category of "public goods." However, I prefer to err on the side of making the category of saleable goods too small rather than too large.

[c] Included in state and local expenditure and should not be counted separately.

[d] Includes some capital expenditures that should not be charged exclusively to current services.

[e] Estimated. 1955 fuels taxes and auto, truck, and bus registration fees were $3.65 billion.

be attributed to higher education. Nevertheless, I believe that nearly everyone agrees that tuition receipts at publicly supported institutions of higher education are less than the costs that reasonably could be allocated to the teaching function.

EDUCATION

As I asserted earlier, the fact that a service has external economies associated with its consumption does not imply that it should not be priced. Consider some of the implications of pricing the services of elementary and secondary schools.

Elementary education is a commodity that is believed to have such important effects upon persons other than those who obtain it that it has been made not only free but compulsory. To make persons pay for something which they may not wish to consume generally would not be considered desirable. However, there may be decided advantages to widening the choice of what might be consumed; and there are potential gains from inducing suppliers to minimize the cost of producing whatever they produce. Combining payments to persons conditional upon these payments being spent upon elementary education with institutional arrangements whereby any entrepreneur who meets certain minimum production requirements is qualified as a seller could further both of these objectives.[2] Adoption of such a proposal would not answer the question, "Are we spending the correct amount upon education?" but it would provide a more satisfactory answer to the question of whether that which was being made available was being provided at minimum cost.

Services that benefit persons other than the immediate users could be offered to users at a price below marginal cost or a subsidy could be provided to users, as was suggested above in the case of elementary education. The latter procedure appears to me to be preferred in that it permits a greater element of competition among suppliers. Thus rather than directly providing innoculations, medical examinations, etc., the government might give each person a minimum grant conditional upon its being used for such purposes and let the person select his own supplier.

Let me now turn to the potentialities of the pricing mechanism

2. See Milton Friedman, "The Role of Government in Education," included in Robert A. Solo, ed., *Economics and the Public Interest*, Rutgers University Press, 1956.

for determining the appropriate production levels for higher education.

The service, higher education, is obtained by consumers because of its impact upon earnings—in which case it can be treated as an investment good—or because the knowledge is desired for its own sake—in which event it can be treated as a consumption good. In either event, I believe that investing in such education is like investing in any other capital asset and that the consumption of higher education by one person does not enter other persons' utility functions.

The statement that one person's consumption of higher education does not enter the utility functions of other persons is an assertion without either adequate proof or disproof.

If my belief is correct, state colleges and universities should receive support from general tax sources only for research; tuition should be raised to cover instruction costs, and the terms under which people can borrow to invest in education should be the same as those under which they can borrow to make other kinds of investments. I am not the sole protagonist of this general proposal and it has by now been widely enough voiced so that I need not develop it further.[3]

We have little information about the demand of educational services so that I can not make a good guess about what the pattern would be if such a proposal were put into effect. However, one would expect the distribution of education to be altered somewhat. Persons now attending college but not willing to pay the full costs would not attend; and persons willing to pay the costs but not now able to obtain funds would attend college. Also one would expect the costs of providing a given level of service to be reduced. Most important of all, the question of whether we need more facilities for higher education could be answered more satisfactorily than it can be at the present time.

Allocating government services by pricing them has limited applicability. To me, an appeal of the price mechanism is that it provides information that would permit us to settle some debates about whether an expenditure is too large or too small. The use of prices in guiding how to produce a given level of service is an area that has not been discussed here. It also offers possibilities for improving resource allocation.

3. See Milton Friedman, *op. cit.*, for example.

Reflections on Public Expenditure Theory

WALTER W. HELLER

Walter W. Heller is Chairman of the President's Council of Economic Advisers. This essay was submitted to the Joint Economic Committee hearings on public expenditures when he was Professor of Economics at the University of Minnesota.

WHAT DOES the economist have to offer a perplexed public and its policymaking representatives on the theory of Government functions as they affect the budget? The cynic's offhand answer, "not much," may be close to the mark if one demands definitive rules of thumb for determining the precise scope of Government functions and level of Government expenditures. But if, instead, the demand is for economic guidelines to aid the budgetary decisionmaker (1) in blending rationally the service, stabilization, and income-transfer functions of Government, (2) in identifying those deficiencies in the private-market mechanism which call for Government budgetary action or, more broadly, those activities where Government use or control of resources promises greater returns than private use or control, and (3) in selecting the most efficient means of carrying out Government functions and activities (whether by Government production, contracts with private producers, transfer payments, loans, guaranties, tax concessions, and so forth)—if this is the nature of the demands on him, the economist is prepared to make a modest offering now and to work along lines that promise a greater contribution in the future.

In a sense, this paper is a progress report designed to show where the economist can already offer some useful counsel, to indicate some of the lines along which promising work is being done, and to suggest certain limitations or constraints within which the economic criteria for dividing resources between public and private use must be applied.

A BASIC FRAMEWORK

As a first step in the search for economic guideposts, we need to disentangle, classify, and define the basic objectives and functions of Government that shape its budgetary decisions. Fortunately, Prof. Richard A. Musgrave has developed a conceptual framework for this task in his "multiple theory of budget determination." [1]

The component functions of the budget as he brings them into focus are: (1) The service, or want-satisfying, function: to provide for the satisfaction of those individual wants which the market mechanism cannot satisfy effectively (e. g., education and conservation) or is incapable of satisfying (e. g., defense and justice); (2) the income-transfer or distributional function: to make those corrections in the existing income distribution (by size, by occupational groups, by geographical area, etc.) which society desires; and (3) the stabilization function: to join with monetary policy and other measures to raise or lower the level of aggregate demand so as to maintain full employment and avoid inflation. The first function is of dominant interest [here] and the succeeding sections of the paper return to it. But several general implications of the Musgrave system as a whole deserve attention before turning to specifics.

Musgrave's formulation helps unclutter our thinking on the component parts of the budget decision. It drives home the significant point that our decisions on how much and what kind of want-satisfying services to provide by Government budgets need not be tied to our demands on the budget for correction of either the existing patterns of income distribution or the level of aggregate demand. If we prefer, we can have a small budget for services (financed by taxes levied on the benefit principle) combined with a big budget for redistributive transfers of income (financed by taxes levied on the ability principle), or vice versa; and either combination can be coupled with either a deficit to stimulate demand and employment or a surplus to reduce demand

1. See, for example, "A Multiple Theory of Budget Determination" *Finanzarchiv* 1957, vol. 13, No. 3, pp. 333–343, and the relevant chapters of his treatise, *The Theory of Public Finance* (New York: McGraw-Hill, 1959).

and check inflation. In this respect, it is reminiscent of Samuelson's "daring doctrine" that by appropriate fiscal-monetary policy "a community can have full employment, can at the same time have the rate of capital formation it wants, and can accomplish all this compatibly with the degree of income-redistributing taxation it ethically desires.[2] Musgrave, in turn, points the way to achieving any combination of Government services, income redistribution, and economic redistribution, and economic stability we set our sights on.

So far, so good. The waters, though deep, are clear and relatively still. They get somewhat muddied and troubled when we move from the clear-cut want-satisfying programs (subject to the benefit principle) and clear-cut distributive programs (subject to the ability principle) into dual-purpose programs, transfers-in-kind in the form of subsidized housing, medical care, vocational education, and so forth. For here we are no longer furnishing services that the majority has voted to meet its own needs (including both selfishly motivated needs like defense and police protection and socially motivated needs like foreign aid) via Government, but are in effect requiring the minority to accept services which they might or might not have bought had they been handed an equivalent amount of cash. Perhaps they would have preferred to spend it on wine, women, and song, but the majority is apparently saying, "No, we know what's best for you." Can this be justified?

It may be digressing to do so, but let us consider for a moment the provision of free vocational education as a case in point. It might be argued that vocational training results in a direct increase in earning power of the trainee (since employers will be willing to pay him higher wages) and that it should therefore be left in private hands or, if furnished publicly, should be financed under the market principle (by direct charges to the recipient of the service) rather than the budget principle (provided free of charge and financed by general taxation).[3] In terms of the service budget alone, the foregoing conclusion is probably

2. Paul A. Samuelson, "The New Look in Tax and Fiscal Policy," in *Federal Tax Policy for Economic Growth and Stability*, Joint Committee on the Economic Report, Washington, November 9, 1955, p. 234.

3. For a discussion of these principles see Gerhard Colm, *Essays in Public Finance and Fiscal Policy*, New York, 1955, pp. 8–11.

right. But bringing in the redistributive motive puts subsidized vocational training in a different light. The voting majority may feel that income transferred in this form constitutes a more efficient and desirable form of transfer than a direct cash transfer. It insures that the transferred economic power won't be squandered in foolish and dissolute ways. It approaches reduction of economic inequality through greater equality of opportunity. In the process, it strengthens the economy's productive capacity.

The new welfare economics may protest that this is a form of tyranny of the majority of the voters over the minority, that each individual is his own best judge of his welfare. Since the equivalent cash payment would have been spent differently, it is said to be a violation of consumer sovereignty. But it is also quite possible that the recipient of the transfer in kind will vote with the majority to have this kind of program rather than a direct cash payment. The individual may accept and welcome the discipline in such an arrangement which overcomes his own self-deplored lack of willpower (a lack which is not restricted to children, aged persons, and imbeciles). How many of us would "prefer" to spend our time quite differently than we do if left to our own devices, yet are willing to accept, or even welcome, the tyranny of a deadline as a condition of participating in a desirable project? Seen in this light, the transfer in kind may interfere more with license than with freedom of consumer choice. I do not mean to dismiss the "tyranny" argument, but its force is certainly softened by the kind of consideration just examined. It may be further softened if we accept the proposition that the responsibility of the voters' representatives goes beyond a mere recording of individual preferences to leadership and education designed to redirect individual preferences along lines which a social consensus deems more constructive.

Even beyond this, the transfer in kind may actually have a large service component, i.e., secondary benefits which accrue to others than the direct recipient of the service.[4] For example,

4. To the extent that the income transfer motive is the sole or dominant motive for keeping certain services on the public budget (or at least causing us to supply them on the budget principle rather than the market principle), a rise in average family income and a decline in inequality will eventually bring us to a point where programs such as vocational education and low-cost housing should be moved off of the Government budget and

low-income housing may confer indirect benefits on high-income people in surrounding areas for which they are willing to pay a considerable price. Subsidized housing projects may replace unsightly slums, arrest urban blight which threatens to encroach on better neighborhoods, and reduce fire and police protection costs. To this extent, taxes on high-income people to subsidize low-cost housing may in large part be a payment for the indirect benefits they receive rather than a transfer payment. Clearly identifying and separating the service elements from the re-distributive element in this manner suggests that the wants of third-party beneficiaries are being satisfied by using the direct recipient of subsidized housing, medical care, education and the like as the instrument, willing or unwilling, for this purpose.

This formulation may also shed new light on the theory of progressive taxation. Musgrave suggests that high-income people may be willing to pay proportionately more for a given government service than low-income people (i.e., the income elasticity of demand for the service is greater than unity), even in the case of government services like defense and justice which by their nature must be consumed in equal amounts by all persons. Add to this consideration the important indirect stake which the upper income groups have in subsidized programs for the lower income groups (i.e., programs not equally consumed by all). The direct beneficiary may put a low value on the service and a high value on money, while the indirect beneficiary (who gets secondary benefits in protection from epidemics, in arresting of urban blight, in a more stable body politic and labor force, and so forth) may put a relatively high value on the service and a low value on money. The tax policy result: progressive taxation on the benefit principle.

---

into the market economy. This point is undoubtedly much more distant for some programs than others. Also, I do not mean to suggest that the main impact of economic growth and prosperity is to reduce Government expenditures. Both in the case of intermediate public goods (such as roads), the demand for which typically moves in accord with private goods, and in the case of "end item" services (such as better education and recrea-tion), the demand for which increases with higher standards of living, economic growth and prosperity mean higher rather than lower demands for Government services. (See Gerhard Colm, "Comments on Samuelson's Theory of Public Finance," *The Review of Economics and Statistics,* November 1956, vol. 38, p. 410.)

ECONOMIC DETERMINANTS OF THE PROPER SPHERE OF GOVERNMENT ACTIVITY

Given a framework for straight thinking about budget functions, the economist is brought face to face with two questions that come closer to the central problem of the proper sphere of Government activity. First, where competitive bidding via the pricing mechanism is inapplicable, how are the preferences of voters for governmental services to be revealed, measured, and appropriately financed? Second, waiving the question of measurement of preferences, where would the line between public and private control over resources be drawn if economic efficiency were the only criterion to be implied?

On the first question, insofar as it relates to individual preferences for public goods, economists have agreed on the nature and difficulty of the problem, have made some intriguing suggestions as to its solution, and have concluded that it is next to insoluble. The key difficulty is that the voting process, unlike the pricing process, does not force the consumer of public goods to show his hand. The essence of preference measurement is the showing of how much of one good or service the consumer is willing to forgo as the price of acquiring another. But the amount of a public good or service (say, of defense, police protection, or schooling) available to the voter is independent of the amount he pays in taxes or the intensity of his demand for it.[5] Unless and until we devise a reliable and reasonably accurate method of detecting specific voter preferences in some detail, our definition of the proper sphere of government activity will have to rely chiefly on the informed judgment and perception of those whom we vote into legislative and executive office.[6]

5. For an illuminating exploration of ways and means to get at a more valid and clear-cut expression of voter preferences for government services, see the pioneering work by Howard R. Bowen, *Toward Social Economy,* New York, 1948, especially ch. 18, "Collective Choice." In this chapter Bowen explores both voting and polling techniques for ascertaining those individual tastes and preferences which cannot find expression in, or be measured by, the market mechanism.

6. Insofar as voter wants in the public sphere go beyond individualistic preferences to general welfare choices (as Colm, in his article commenting on Samuelson's theory, argues that they not only do, but should), the

This being the case, the economist's task is to contribute what he can to this informed judgment and perception. In effect, the economist's job becomes one of telling the voters and their representatives what their preferences as to governmental activities would be if they were guided by the principle of economic efficiency. In doing so, the economist is not proposing that decisions as to what kinds of activities should be assigned to government—what wants should be satisfied and resources should be redirected through government action—should be made on economic grounds alone. He is fully aware that values such as those of political and economic freedom play a vital role in these decisions. But he can perform the valuable service of identifying those deficiencies in the market mechanism and those inherent economic characteristics of government which make it economically advantageous to have certain services provided by government rather than by private initiative. In other words he can show where government intervention in resource allocation and use promises a greater return per unit of input than untrammeled private use.

The economist recognizes, of course, that there are areas in which he is necessarily mute, or at least should not speak unless spoken to. These are the areas of pure public goods, whose benefits are clearly indivisible and nonmarketable, and no amount of economic wisdom can determine the appropriate levels of output and expenditure.[7] In the realm of defense, for example, one successful Russian earth satellite or intercontinental ballistics missile will (and should), outweigh 10,000 economists in determining the appropriate level of expenditures. At most, the

---

problem changes form, but the desirability of sharper definition of voter preferences remains undiminished.

7. No attempt is made here to define a public good. Samuelson (in "The Pure Theory of Public Expenditures," *The Review of Economics and Statistics*, November 1954, vol. 36, p. 387) has defined "collective consumption goods" as those in which one individual's consumption of the good leads to no diminution of any other individual's consumption of that good. McKenna [in an unpublished paper.—*Editor*] would broaden the definition to include as public goods all those that provide "benefit simultaneously and automatically to more than one member of society." It would seem that while the former definition leaves out many goods provided under the budget principle, McKenna's embraces quite a number provided under the market principle. [For a discussion of public goods see the essay by Bator in this volume. *Editor.*]

economist stands ready to offer analysis and judgments as to the critical levels of defense expenditures beyond which they threaten serious inflation in the absence of drastic tax action or curtailment of civilian programs, or, given that action, threaten impairment of producer incentives and essential civilian programs.

A much more fruitful activity for the economist is to demonstrate the economic advantage offered by government intervention, budgetary and otherwise, in those intermediate service areas where benefits are at least partially divisible and marketable. A number of economists have made useful contributions on this front.[8] In what situations does economic logic point to government intervention to correct the market mechanism's allocation of resources in the interests of greater efficiency in their use?

1. Where there are important third-party benefits [usually known as neighborhood effects, external effects, or externalities] which accrue to others than the direct beneficiary of the service as in the case of education, disease prevention, police and fire protection, the market price and demand schedules underestimate the marginal and total social benefits provided by the service in question. By and large, the direct beneficiaries are the only ones who enter the private market as buyers, with the result that the services would be undervalued, underpriced, and underproduced unless Government entered the transaction. Government is the instrument for representing the third-party beneficiaries and correcting the deficiency of the market place (though this is not to deny that private religious and philanthropic organizations, for example, also represent third-party beneficiaries and operate on budget rather than market principles).

2. Just as there may be indirect benefits not reflected in market demand, there may be indirect costs inflicted on society which do not enter the private producer's costs and therefore do not influence market supply. Classic examples are the costs of smog,

8. See, for example, O. H. Brownlee and E. D. Allen, *Economics of Public Finance*, second edition, New York, 1954, ch. 10, "The Role of Government Expenditure." See also Max F. Millikan, "Objectives for Economic Policy in a Democracy" (especially pp. 62–68), and Robert Dahl and Charles E. Lindblom, "Variation in Public Expenditure," both in *Income Stabilization for a Developing Democracy*, Max F. Millikan, editor, New Haven, 1953.

water pollution, denuding of forests, and the like. In these areas, private output will exceed the optimum level unless government corrects the situation either by regulation or by a combination of expenditure and charge-backs to the private producers involved.

3. Where a service is best provided, for technical reasons, as a monopoly (e.g., postal service, electricity, railroad transportation), the Government is expected to step in either by regulation or operation to avoid costly duplication and improve the quality of service. Ideally, its function would also be to guide prices toward levels consistent with optimum output. Involved here is the problem of the decreasing cost industry, where efficient plant size is so large relative to total demand that average cost decreases as output increases, and the market solution of the output and price problem will not result in best use of the productive assets. To push production to a point representing an ideal use of resources may require, if not Government operation, a subsidy financed out of tax revenues.

4. Government may enjoy some advantages in production or distribution which make it an inherently more efficient producer of certain services. Here, the classic case is highways, streets, and sidewalks. By providing them free to all comers, Government effects substantial savings in costs of distribution since it does not have to meter the service and charge a price for each specific use. In this category we might also fit projects, such as the initial development of atomic energy, which involve such great risks and huge accumulations of capital that the private market does not have the financial tools to cope with them.

ALTERNATIVE MEANS OF CARRYING OUT GOVERNMENT FUNCTIONS

Given the decisions as to the appropriate sphere of Government activity (on the basis not merely of considerations of greatest economic gain but also of value preferences), there remains the problem of choice among alternative methods to implement these decisions, to achieve given aims and satisfy expressed public wants. This choice will affect the budget in different ways. It may increase expenditures, decrease revenues, establish contingent liabilities, or perhaps have no effect on the budget at all (except for a small amount of administrative expenses involved in the supervisory and regulatory activities). Since the operational question is not merely what functions and activities Government should carry out, but what budgetary principles and expenditure levels these lead to, the problem of implementation must be included in any applied theory of public expenditures.

Here, the economist's role is to determine the most efficient method of providing the service or otherwise influencing resource allocation. He is concerned with minimizing costs, i.e., achieving the stated objective with a minimum expenditure of resources. Needless to say, other considerations will also influence the selection among alternative means, as even a brief consideration of the types of choices involved in the implementation process will make clear.

What are these choices? Take first the case of direct satisfaction of individuals' public wants. Should the Government produce the desired public goods or obtain them from private industry by purchase or contract? To accomplish redistributive ends, should the Government provide transfers in cash or transfers in kind? [9] Should Government rely on public production of educational services, or should it consider private production combined with earmarked transfers of purchasing power to parents? Thus far, the choices all involve direct budgetary expenditures, the level of which differs, at least marginally, depending on the relative efficiency of the method chosen. But in making his choice, the policymaker must consider not merely the direct costs of providing the service but whether one method involves more or less disturbance of private market incentives and patterns of production than another, whether it involves more or less interference with individual freedom (which is largely a function of the extent of Government expenditures and intervention but certainly in part also a function of the form of that intervention), and so on.

Another set of choices may take the item off of the expenditure

9. One involves so-called resource-using (also called factor-purchase or exhaustive) Government expenditures, i.e., payments in exchange for current goods and services rendered, with direct control of resources remaining in public hands. The other involves transfer payments, i.e., payments made without any provision of current goods and services in return, with direct control over resources passing into private hands. [The distinction is discussed in the Introduction to this volume. *Editor.*]

side of the budget entirely, or leave it there only contingently. Should such subsidies as those to promote oil and gas exploration, stimulate foreign investment, expand the merchant marine, promote low-cost housing, and increase the flow of strategic minerals take the form of (1) outright subsidies or above-market-price purchase programs, (2) Government loan programs, (3) Government guaranties, or (4) tax concessions? The choice will clearly involve quite different impacts on Government expenditures.

In many of these cases, the economist can be helpful with his efficiency criterion. But one would be naive to think that efficiency alone dictates the choice. The economist may show that a direct subsidy could stimulate a given amount of private direct investment abroad or a given amount of exploration for oil and gas, with a much smaller cost to the budget than is implicitly required in the tax concession method of achieving the same end. Yet, the costlier tax concession method may be preferred for two simple reasons: (1) it is virtually self-administering, involving no administrative hierarchy to substitute its authority for relatively free private decisions, and (2) it does not involve an increase in the expenditure side of the budget, a fact which has certain attractions to the Executive and Congress.

As yet, no clear boundary lines have been drawn among the various forms of Government intervention to mark off those that properly belong within the scope of public expenditure theory. But this illustrative review of the various choices makes clear that some forms of Government activity which are not reflected in expenditures at all (tax concessions) or only contingently (guaranties) are an integral part of such expenditure theory. In fact, there may be a stronger case for embracing these in expenditure theory than many Government activities which require budgetary outlays but are conducted on the pricing principle, i.e., Government enterprise activities.

Economists are conducting some provocative inquiries into questions of alternative methods of carrying out Government programs in areas where the answers had heretofore been taken for granted. For example, the transfer of schooling to a private production and Government transfer payment basis has been urged by Professor Milton Friedman as a more efficient means of providing the desired service.[10] Professor O. H. Brownlee is currently probing further into this question, as well as the possibilities of transferring other publicly produced services into the sphere of private production.[11] Once fairly conclusive findings are devised as to the methods most likely to minimize costs, there remains the vital task of blending these findings with the nonmonetary values that would be gained or lost in the process of transferring from public to private production.

SOME CONSTRAINTS ON THE APPLICATION OF SPECIFIC ECONOMIC CRITERIA

Repeatedly in this discussion, the note has been sounded that, in determining the level of Government activity, the policymaker cannot live by economics alone. More particularly, we need to guard against setting up our economic guides solely in terms of those considerations which lend themselves to sharp economic analysis and definition. In other words, the role of both economic and noneconomic constraints must be given full weight.

The former include a host of considerations relating particularly to economic motivation in Government versus private undertakings. Government may, for example, have a decided edge in the efficiency of distribution or be able to achieve a better balancing of social costs and social benefits in a variety of fields. Yet, there may be important offsets to these economic advantages in terms of (1) bureaucracy, (2) lack of the profit criterion to gage the results of Government activities, and (3) undesigned or unintended (presumably adverse) economic effects of taxation.[12]

10. See Milton Friedman, "The Role of Government in Education," in *Economics and The Public Interest*, Robert A. Solo, editor, New Brunswick, 1955, pp. 123–144. In his prescription, Friedman would, of course, have Government regulate the private schools to the extent of insuring that they meet certain minimum standards in their programs and facilities.

11. [See the essay by Brownlee included in this volume for his analysis of government roles in education. *Editor.*]

12. These less sharply defined economic effects have to be balanced, of course, against comparable and perhaps offsetting drawbacks in the market mechanism. For an exploration of some of these factors, both in the private and the public sphere, see Robert A. Dahl and Charles E. Lindblom, *Politics, Economics, and Welfare*, New York, 1953, especially pt. V. See also C. Lowell Harriss, "Government Spending: Issues of Theory and Practices," *Public Finance*, vol. 12, 1957, pp. 7–19.

The latter factor, in particular the fact that tax financing of public services involves breaking the link between an individual's cost of a given service and his benefit from it, may involve important offsets to economic advantages otherwise gained by Government expenditure. Thus far, to be sure, no dire consequences of the disincentive effects of taxation have been firmly proved, but changes in the form of private economic activity to minimize taxes are certainly a cost that must be weighed when netting out the balance of economic advantage in Government versus private performance of services.

Beyond the economic factors, one encounters an even more basic and less manageable constraint, namely that of freedom of choice. Thus, it is quite conceivable that following the kinds of economic criteria discussed earlier in the paper would take us considerably farther in the direction of Government spending and control over resource allocation than we would wish to go in terms of possible impairment of economic and political freedom. This consideration enters importantly not merely in decisions as to the proper range of Government activity but also in choosing among alternative methods of providing Government services.

This is not to imply that all value considerations run counter to the expansion of the Government sector of our economy. Such expansion may serve a number of social values, such as greater equality of income and opportunity, a more acceptable social environment, and so on.[13]

To get all of these considerations into the decision-making equation on private versus public provision of a particular service, or on the choice among alternative forms of providing the service, requires a wisdom which goes well beyond the field of economics. Perhaps this explains why so few economists enter politics.

13. This type of consideration is examined in William Vickrey, "An Exchange of Questions Between Economics and Philosophy," in *Goals of Economic Life*, edited by A. Dudley Ward, New York, 1953, pp. 148–177. See also Max F. Millikan, op. cit.

The Tenable Range of Functions of
Local Government

GEORGE J. STIGLER

*George J. Stigler is Walgreen Professor of American Institutions
at the University of Chicago. He was one of the panelists appearing before a Congressional subcommittee who contributed papers to the compendium* Federal Expenditures for Growth and
Stability.

The members of the legislative, executive, and judiciary departments
of 13 and more States, the justices of peace, officers of militia, minis-
terial officers of justice, with all the county, corporation, and town
officers, for 3 million and more of people, intermixed, and having particular acquaintance with every class and circle of people, must exceed, beyond all proportion, both in number and influence, those of
every description who will be employed in the administration of the
Federal system (*The Federalist,* No. 45).

THE PRESERVATION of a large role in governmental activity for
local governments is widely accepted as an important social goal.
No one can doubt that the individual citizen gains greatly in
political dignity and wisdom if he can participate in the political
process beyond casting a vote periodically. It is also generally
conceded that a good political system adapts itself to the differing
circumstances and mores of different localities, or, as I would
wish to rephrase it, the system should allow legitimate variations
of types and scales of governmental activity to correspond with
variations in the preferences of different groups of citizens.

Nor will it be denied that this social goal is being increasingly
sacrificed. In 1900, virtually all questions of housing, public
health, crime, and local transportation were dealt with exclusively by State or local governments, and the role of the
Federal Government in education, regulation of business practices, control of natural resources, and redistribution of income

was negligible. Today the Federal Government is very active in each of these areas, and its share of responsibility is gradually increasing.

I propose to examine some of the reasons which are given for the growing centralization of political processes. The proper range of activities of government in general will not be raised. Our question is simply this: If the people in a given community wish to embark on a particular governmental policy, when does the efficient discharge of this policy require that it be imposed by a central authority also upon other communities?

In many minor areas of governmental activity no real questions are raised, as yet, about the feasibility of local sovereignty. If a given community wishes to have superb library facilities, it can build and pay for them; if another community wishes instead a skating rink, it may so choose. If individual citizens in any community disagree strongly with the majority preferences, they may move to a more congenial community. Since governmental functions must often be provided upon a considerable scale to be tolerably efficient in execution, a sufficiently eccentric individual may not be able to find any community with enough like-minded individuals to be able to adopt that series of governmental policies which would exactly suit his taste. For example, he may wish to live in a community with gravel streets and a magnificent observatory, and find no community willing to provide this combination. This sort of limitation is also encountered in consuming the products of private enterprise—I may not find precisely the automobile or typewriter that suits me.

In most areas of governmental activity, however, it is increasingly felt that local governments are inefficient units. When any of three types of governmental activity are sought, it is said that the unit of effective administration must be large in scale—

1. When the object of a regulatory policy can be nullified by the competition of (including migration to) other local governmental units.

2. When the source of revenue of the activity can escape financial responsibility by migration to another unit.

3. When the policy is incapable of efficient performance upon a local scale.

We consider these problems in turn.

THE PROBLEM OF COMPETITION

Suppose that a community wishes to set a high standard of factory safety, and requires the installation of a very expensive safety device. Then the local portion of a much larger industry will be undersold in the common market by factories in other communities, provided they do not also simultaneously set as high standards of safety practices. The local branch of the industry then dies or migrates. These facts can be taken as data for our discussion.

The essence of this argument is that competition, which usually works so well in the area of private enterprise, serves to defeat desirable goals in the area of government. If every governmental unit, save one, were to desire and require elaborate safety devices in the factories of some industry, it is claimed that their desire could be stultified by the presence of the exceptional community which did not have this desire, because the regulated industry would migrate to this community and escape regulation, and the knowledge that it would do so is often enough to prevent the various communities from attempting to regulate it.

It may be remarked that a similar argument is often encountered in the private-enterprise sector. Plants with low wage rates, it is often said, force plants with high wage rates to reduce their wages in order to compete successfully in the common market. In this case the argument is reversible: the plants with high wage rates force plants with low wage rates to raise their wages in order to compete successfully for workers in the common labor market. Both formulations, however, are singularly uninformative, for they do not lead directly to the correct conclusion, which is that the wages of all (similar) workers must approach equality in all plants under competition, and the common wage rate will be governed by the value of the worker's services in those plants which can pay this rate. Can it be that some parallel obscurity attaches to the customary formulation of the unfortunate effect of competition among governments?

The governmental analysis is, in fact, incomplete. Suppose any community set the required level of safety practices as high as it wishes, and then gave a subsidy to each enterprise in the locality equal to the additional cost that these safety devices imposed upon the enterprises. Then there would be no tendency for the local industry to be handicapped in competition with other areas with lower safety standards, and the community would enjoy more worker safety and less of other things than other communities. If 47 percent of the localities or 99 percent of the localities embark upon this policy, then 47 or 99 percent of the factories will have the desired safety practices, and the nonconformist competitors will not have the slightest tendency to injure or attract these safe and expensive factories.

When a community imposes the safety regulations without giving a compensating subsidy, its troubles arise from the fact that it is seeking to push these higher costs off on consumers, and neither local nor distant consumers wish to assume this burden. The problem of competition resolves itself into an unwillingness of the community to bear the costs of its policy when they are posed as an explicit burden.

A similar analysis holds when the community wishes to require of some consumer good that it be of unusually high quality. If it specifies that only goods of this unusual quality be sold in the community, the producers will be quite eager to meet the specifications—at a remunerative price.

Although it involves a digression, it may be profitable to discuss more generally our example of factory safety devices because the discussion will serve to illuminate the workings of competition in general. If workers are faced with the choice of working in one plant, unequipped with safety devices, at an hourly rate of $1.50 but with expected losses from injuries of 5 cents per hour, and in another plant with safety devices they are offered $1.46 with no expected losses from injuries, we should expect them to choose the latter plant. If under these conditions they do not choose the safer plant, the most probable explanation is that they do not correctly appraise the expected losses from injuries and the remedy is to inform them of the consequences of working in factories unequipped with safety devices. In a fully competitive system the entrepreneurs will supply at cost all the safety devices that the workers demand, and all safety devices which return (to the worker, in terms of reduced injuries) as much or more than the cost will be adopted. It may well be that in this situation there will be safety devices which do not pay but which would reduce injuries further, and that the community as a whole sets a higher value on avoidance of these injuries than the workers themselves do. Some moral philosophers might argue that these workers should set a higher value on the avoidance of injuries, but the workers do not, and in a society with free choice of occupation they cannot be made to pay for more safety than they wish. Hence the society must bear the costs of achieving more safety, and the sole question is whether the costs be borne by consumers through compulsory installation of the safety devices and restriction of supply, or by direct grant from public funds.

The competition of other communities as tax collectors is an important form of the alleged difficulty arising out of competition. Suppose community A wishes to have splendid and expensive schools, streets, housing, poor relief, and what not. If it levies sufficient taxes to finance this elaborate program, a large portion of the tax base (industries and well-to-do individuals) will leave the community while simultaneously a large number of beneficiaries of the generous program may immigrate. The tax rates on the narrower tax base will have to be prohibitive (from the viewpoint of the remaining taxpayers) to finance the sumptuous program.

Again we can accept the facts, with one temporary amendment. Let us assume that the same income is received by every family, and no questions of income redistribution are involved. Will the presence of communities with lower tax rates defeat the ambitions of community A? The answer is clearly in the negative. There will be some redistribution of population among communities: those people who prefer cheaper public services and lower tax rates will move elsewhere, and others with opposite taste will move to A. Competition of communities offers not obstacles but opportunities to various communities to choose the types and scales of governmental functions they wish. The proviso that all family incomes are equal has a vast influence on this argument, of course, and we turn now to income redistribution as a goal.

THE DISTRIBUTION OF INCOME

If all families had equal (real) income, would there be any need for local governmental units? Why could not each city be a private corporation, supplying at a price the services its dwellers demanded? With many, many such corporations, competition would prevent monopolistic pricing, and schooling and police and fire protection would be sold at a price including a fair rate of return on investment. This scheme would obviously be inappropriate where the service must be a monopoly (like national defense) and probably also where the community size was so large (due to the economic advantages of size) that the communities were too few to rely upon competition, but let us put these instances aside. We are not seeking to prove that there should be no government, but rather to find the logic of government at the multiunit governmental level.

A basic deficiency in this private-enterprise organization of social life, we would all agree, is that it allows excessive freedom to the individual. It would allow parents to horsewhip children, and it would create communities populated chiefly with drunkards and drug addicts—although thieves would presumably prefer to live among honest men (even with their policemen) than only with other thieves. Public opinion would curb many undesirable personal actions, but the society would wish to compel observance of its basic values. As a result, we must recognize the need for political units large enough so their numbers include enough normal people to insure the imposition of the society's basic moral standards on local communities. Our States —with one or two possible western exceptions—meet this condition of statistical large numbers.

The second basic weakness—some will call it a strength—of the private enterprise organization of local government is that it would not permit price discrimination; it does not have the ability to redistribute income. The purely competitive organization of local services would make it impossible for a local government to obtain money from the rich to pay for the education of the children of the poor, except to the extent that the rich voluntarily assumed this burden.

How can local governments cope with this problem? If 99 communities tax the rich to aid the poor, the rich may congregate in the hundredth community, so this uncooperative community sets the tune. Here competition does not perform with its usual excellence, for competition is the system calculated to organize only voluntary activity.

What is the correct amount of redistribution of income in light of the society's desires? It is more than the unrestricted competition of tax-free colonies of the rich would allow, but less than the most aggressively egalitarian community would desire. The decision must be in some sense a national decision, for the proper amount of redistribution, even if rich and poor were chained to their communities, could not depend upon the accidents of income composition of a particular community. And once this level of redistribution is set, no one community may complain if its rich citizens migrate when it seeks to go above this level of distribution unless the society is prepared to let the most egalitarian community set the scale of income redistribution.

Since redistribution is intrinsically a national policy, it should not be restricted to a community level; a community consisting only of poor people should receive the desired minimum social services. Hence, in pure principle, the Federal Government should collect the progressive levies and redistribute them (in whole or in part) to local units with each unit receiving an amount governed by the number of its poor and the degree of their poverty.

Given this system of tax revenue redistribution, the local governments could still be allowed to perform any function which they were competent to perform efficiently. One community might choose to spend more on schools and less on hospitals than another, but this is surely an area of legitimate freedom; there is no "correct" distribution of expenditures among such functions.

In a society which has no serious program of income redistribution (even as a means to the attainment of minimum goals), local governments would face no basic revenue problems because of competition.[1] It is in keeping with this argument that a century ago almost all functions were local and the problem of competition for the tax base was negligible. With an appropriate fiscal system we could restore these revenue considerations to a position of unimportance even in an era of extensive income redistribution. There still remains the question of whether the local governments could efficiently perform the enlarged range of functions that modern governments have assumed. We turn now to this question.

1. Perhaps a qualification should be entered with respect to the growth of taxable wealth that escapes a general property tax. In England the desire of property owners to ease their tax burdens was a force in the emasculation of local government; see E. Cannan, *The History of Local Rates in England,* second edition, 1912, ch. VI.

THE ECONOMIES OF SCALE

How large must a governmental unit be to perform efficiently the activities which the public wishes governments to perform? This is an area which deserves much more attention than it appears to have received, and the following remarks are highly tentative.

There is a set of functions which are intrinsically national because they are indivisible. The greatest of these is national defense, and it would be ill-served if each State or local unit were to undertake the defense of its own area. One may cite also foreign relations, the national governmental machinery, and the control of relationships among lower governmental levels.

In addition to such traditional functions, one may list certain functions which are or can be performed at a local level but which must be coordinated to achieve efficiency in their design. The transportation systems of localities must take some account also of the needs of long-distance transportation. The radio and television stations of various localities must not jam one another. These are functions which in the economist's language, have large external economies or diseconomies accruing to the areas which do not participate in their execution, so it is essential that they be formulated (although not necessarily administered) on a larger area than the local government.

We should reserve for the Federal Government those functions which are much more efficiently discharged on the largest scale. When local performance involves large duplication, it is inefficient. Thus it seems undesirable to have 48 estimates of wholesale prices since the price movements in most regions will be parallel; on the other hand, the calculation of cost-of-living indexes might suitably be removed from the Bureau of Labor Statistics to the States.

The optimum scale of performance has tacitly become identified with the National, or at least the State, scale almost without examining the nature of the governmental functions under discussion. This seems most surprising to the student of industrial organization; he is accustomed to finding that the activity in an industry with a complex technology is usually efficiently conducted by a firm smaller by almost any measure than the government of a town of 25,000. Is there some special characteristic of governmental functions that makes large units necessary to efficiency?

Only one characteristic seems a possible candidate for this role: the great variety of functions performed by even the small governmental units. The lack of specialization is pronounced even though political scientists complain of a multiplicity of overlapping local units (many of which were established to evade tax or debt limits on local units). Some of these functions can be performed efficiently on a very small scale. Many of the most distinguished private schools and colleges are much smaller than the school system of a town of 5,000 people. Others are more varied. A police department can efficiently control local traffic on a small scale; in one sense it must be worldwide to have an efficient "missing persons" bureau.

But this variety of function is not really unusual. Every enterprise must use goods and services, or produce goods or services, which must be produced or sold on a much wider scale than the enterprise itself can undertake. Even a huge department store is not large enough to make its own delivery trucks, or to print the newspapers in which it advertises. Just as cooperation in these matters is brought about by the price system, so cooperation among governmental units has been developed—and could be carried much further—to avoid the determination and execution of all public functions by that governmental unit which is most efficient in conducting the function with the largest scale of operation.

It happens, as we have already noticed, that one function of paramount importance must be conducted on a very large scale: the collection of revenues designed to redistribute income. Much centralization, in fact probably most centralization, has been a consequence of this situation. A central government is loath to make grants without exercising a degree of control over the local units which disburse the funds. No degree of control less than 100 percent, however, is sufficient to guarantee local performance exactly as the central authorities wish it, and there is no obstacle except tradition to slow down their gradual extension of controls.

The case for imposing controls over the smaller units receiving grants, however, is far from general. The central disbursing authority has no monopoly of wisdom. The State boards of education have imposed a series of certification requirements on local teachers, for example, that have done much to lower the quality of elementary education in the United States. When central governments have superior civil servants, as they often do, the cause lies more often in their control of finance and authority than in the advantages of centralization. It may be true that when most administrative units are small the ablest men cannot conduct affairs on the largest scale, but this seems an odd consideration to give weight in setting the functions of local governments in a democracy. More often the complexity of the tasks at the national level has reached such levels that not the ablest men can control them efficiently.

If grants were given to local governments without supervision, there would be some instances of gross neglect or venality and more variety in the quality of the performance of public functions. We should also expect to find that much of this variety was eminently sensible, and that many types of experimentation would constantly be embarked upon by the more venturesome and the more foolish communities—with large social benefits from both the successes and the failures.

If we give each governmental activity to the smallest governmental unit which can efficiently perform it, there will be a vast resurgence and revitalization of local government in America. A vast reservoir of ability and imagination can be found in the increasing leisure time of the population, and both public functions and private citizens would benefit from the increased participation of citizens in political life. An eminent and powerful structure of local government is a basic ingredient of a society which seeks to give to the individual the fullest possible freedom and responsibility.

Suggested Further Readings

American Assembly, *Atoms for Power* (Prentice-Hall, 1958).

Bator, Francis M., *The Question of Government Spending* (Harper, 1960).

Baumol, William J., *Welfare Economics and the Theory of State* (Harvard, 1952).

Black, Duncan, *The Theory of Committees and Elections* (Cambridge, 1958).

Bowen, Howard R., *Toward Social Economy* (Rinehart, 1948).

Break, George F., "Income Tax and Incentives to Work: An Empirical Study," *American Economic Review*, September 1957.

Brownlee, O. H. and W. W. Heller, "Highway Development and Financing," *American Economic Review*, May 1956.

Buchanan, James M., "Politics, Policy and Pigovian Margins," *Economica*, February 1962.

Clark, John M., *Alternative to Serfdom* (Knopf, 1948).

Committee for Economic Development, *The Budget and Economic Growth* (1958).

————, *Paying for Better Public Schools* (1959).

————, *Guiding Metropolitan Growth* (1960).

Dahl, Robert A. and Charles E. Lindblom, *Politics, Economics and Welfare* (Harper, 1953).

Davis, Otto A. and Andrew B. Whinston, "The Economics of Urban Renewal," *Law and Contemporary Problems* (Winter 1961).

Fabricant, Solomon, *The Trend of Government Activity in the United States Since 1900* (National Bureau of Economic Research, 1952).

Fellner, William J., "Politics, Economics and Recession," *Yale Review*, 1959.

Friedman, Milton, "The Role of Government in Education," *Economics and the Public Interest*, ed., R. Solo (Rutgers, 1955).

Galbraith, J. K., *The Affluent Society* (Houghton Mifflin, 1958).

Gulick, Luther H., *The Metropolitan Problem and American Ideas* (Knopf, 1962).

Hansen, Alvin H., *Economic Issues of the 1960's* (McGraw-Hill, 1961).

Hayek, F., *The Road to Serfdom* (Chicago, 1944).

Hirschleifer, Jack, J. C. DeHaven, J. W. Milliman, *Water Supply: Economics, Technology and Policy* (Chicago, 1960).

Hitch, Charles J. and R. N. McKean, *The Economics of Defense in the Nuclear Age* (Harvard, 1960).

Keezer, Dexter, ed., *Financing Higher Education, 1960–1970* (McGraw-Hill, 1959).

Krutilla, John V., and Otto Eckstein, *Multiple Purpose River Development* (Johns Hopkins, 1958).

Lerner, Abba P., *The Economics of Control* (Macmillan, 1944).

Machlup, Fritz, "The Division of Labor Between Government and Private Enterprise," *American Economic Review,* March Supplement, 1943.

McKean, Roland N., *Efficiency in Government through Systems Analysis* (Wiley, 1958).

Musgrave, Richard A., *The Theory of Public Finance* (McGraw-Hill, 1959).

The Nation and Its Industry in Space, special June 1962 issue of *Fortune.*

Rivlin, Alice M., *The Role of the Federal Government in Financing Higher Education* (Brookings, 1962).

Rothenberg, Jerome, *The Measurement of Social Welfare* (Prentice-Hall, 1961).

Samuelson, Paul A., "Diagrammatic Exposition of a Theory of Public Expenditure," *Review of Economics and Statistics,* November 1955.

Schumpeter, J. A., *Capitalism, Socialism and Democracy,* 3rd edn. (Harper, 1953).

Shenfield, A. A., "The Public Sector versus the Private Sector in Britain," *Modern Age, 6,* No. 1 (Winter 1961–2).

Simon, Herbert A., and Clarence E. Ridley, "The Criterion of Efficiency," *Annals of the American Academy of Political and Social Science,* September 1938.

Somers, Herman M. and Anne R., *Doctors, Patients and Health Insurance* (Brookings, 1961).

Tiebout, Charles M., "A Pure Theory of Local Expenditures," *Journal of Political Economy,* October 1956.

Tullock, Gordon, "Problems of Majority Voting," *Journal of Political Economy,* December 1959.

Turnbull, John G., C. A. Williams and E. F. Cheit, *Economic and Social Security,* 2nd edn. (Ronald, 1962).

U.S. Congress, Joint Economic Committee, *Federal Expenditure Policy for Growth and Stability* (1957).

Wallich, Henry G., *The Costs of Freedom* (Harper, 1960).

Weisbrod, Burton A., *The Economics of Public Health* (Pennsylvania, 1962).